FORTUNE AND [illegible] N

A History of Lubboc[illegible], Chislehurst

A personal journey
by
JOANNA FRIEL

OCBC

Old Chapel Books, Chislehurst

Published in Great Britain by
Old Chapel Books, Chislehurst,
The Old Chapel, Queens Passage, Chislehurst, BR7 5AP

First published, July 2018

Paperback ISBN 978-1-912236-07-7

Printed in Great Britain by
CPI Antony Rowe
Eastbourne
East Sussex
BN23 6PE

The photograph on the front cover is of a painting by Robert A Muller commissioned in 1877. It shows the five children of Francis John Johnston (1831-1911) and his wife Caroline Earle (d.1875).
From left to right:
Horace James (1866-1915), Caroline Margaret(1867-1926), Harriet Monica (1870-1927), Violet Mary (1868-1942) and Francis Alexander (1864-1958)
The house, Lamas, can be seen between Violet and Francis.
The photograph is reproduced by kind permisson of the owner, the grandson of Horace James.

Contents

Introduction iii

1. The Camden Park Estate 1
2. Lamas 9
3. Raggleswood 27
4. Oakbank 33
5. Camden Hill 47
6. Coed-bel 53
7. Granite Lodge 63
8. Christ Church 71
9. Ravensbrook 77
10. The Arab's Tent 85
11. Camden Lodge 93
12. The Rookery 105
13. Abbey Lodge and Hillside 119
14. Beechcroft 127
15. Claverley 135
16. The Great War 141
17. Seven Trees (originally Rosedale) 151
18. St Hugh's School/ Mount Zion 161
19. The Flood 165

Conclusions 173

Dedicated to
My Dad, Alistair Sinton 1927 – 2017
who gave me my love of local history

Introduction

'Chislehurst is one of the most pleasant and healthy villages among the many, that lie within the environs of the metropolis, and has within its bounds ... numbers of elegant villas, with gardens and plantations beautifully disposed. These are dispersed throughout the village, and around the Common, and are in general inhabited by persons of fortune and distinction.'

Hasted, *History of Kent*, 1778.

Finding out about those persons of fortune and distinction all began over a cup of coffee! I have been fortunate enough to meet many distinctive and generous people over cups of coffee, as well as tea, lunch and, particularly in Paris, several glasses of wine! The stories I have discovered about the lives of the residents of Lubbock Road have included tea and coffee purveyors, but mostly purveyors of services: bankers, doctors and lawyers, but also engineers, photographers, clerics, a blind architect and a couple of MPs. These are the ones who made their fortune; there are those who earned distinction with daring and bravery: missionaries, a suffragette, First World War nurses and a tale involving our very own Schindler, Lord Nicholas Winton, who rescued Jewish children from Prague in 1938.

I retired in 2009, having rather tired myself out continuing to work following a diagnosis of multiple sclerosis back in 2001. So-called retirement enabled me to really begin my research into the Lubbock name. When you live in a road named after a person, there is a need to have knowledge about that individual. (I just didn't realise then quite what a journey that knowledge was going to take me on!)

Conducting the research has been such a pleasure; for me, certainly, less so perhaps for my family. My eldest daughter at one stage called me a stalker but had I not put that letter through an unknown person's door I would never have learned about 'Tubby', who lived in my own house and left thousands of pounds to a Zimbabwe scholarship fund. Had I not written to the neighbours I didn't know, I would never have found the books and photographs of John Lubbock's home; and if I hadn't clicked on other people's family trees on Ancestry.com, I would never have known that Brian Johnston, the cricket commentator, had a link to a family in this road.

My son became most perturbed when I kept referring, on Facebook at least, to 'my dead boy'. This was Gerald Harwood, one of the First World War casualties, who, I discovered, lived in our very own house. Imagine my shock, if you will, when reading his story in Yvonne Auld's local history book *For King and Country*; I realised that this boy, only 24 at the time of his death, had probably played in my garden, eaten in my dining room and I was very likely reading of his demise in the room that had been his own bedroom.

My youngest daughter has been ever patient: answering the front door and telephone to curious folk that neither of us knew but all of whom were essential to the fabric of the stories that unfolded. I don't think she minded so much when the stories involved the odd glass of wine which kept her mother quiet, for a little while, at least!

The journey has taken me, virtually, far and wide: within the UK to Dundee and Edinburgh, Southport and Birmingham; abroad to Ireland, Africa, Japan and Hong Kong; and then physically (no mean feat for me) and hilariously to Paris. Really distinctive names from Victorian Britain have popped up: Charles Darwin, General Gordon of Khartoum and Cardinal Manning, and other names that ought to be distinctive but have not stood the test of time, namely John Lubbock, from whom the road takes its name.

It's not all been about men, either; there are deeply moving stories of the female residents, too. The stifling strictures, pains and frustrations endured by these women, namely Ellen Lubbock, Caroline Johnston, Emily Wood and Ellen Silver: baby factories, all corsets and calling cards, distinctive lives, certainly, but perhaps not so fortunate.

I have tried to tell the story of the road through the great houses and the many lives led inside them and have aimed to tell that story at least through to 1939, with a glimpse at the time beyond.

The coffee I mentioned at the start was at an open morning at Christ Church, the beautiful Church of England establishment just 500 yards down the road from where I lived. We moved into Lubbock Road just after the millennium and naturally I wanted to meet the neighbours. The Church event was a great place to start and I noticed in the hall a sepia aerial photograph of the area. Michael Adams, the then vicar, soon to be Canon, said I was welcome to borrow it to see it more clearly. I gingerly removed it from its frame to discover the name of the company on the reverse and joy of joys (the first of many exciting finds for me) a contact number. Of course, I picked up the phone and, amazingly, they were still in business and, even more amazingly, they had other images they could send. I think this was the first of many purchases made in the name of discovery, but such a worthwhile one. The picture they sent showed my own house, along with the other period houses in the road. In 1890, there were 23 grand Victorian piles in Lubbock Road; now only 11 historic buildings remain, with many blocks of flats in the place of the others.

On the face of it, Lubbock Road seems just a pleasant, ordinary road in a leafy area, but fortunately I have uncovered some genuinely distinctive characters. I just had to find out who had lived here. These are some of the stories that have unfolded.

In putting this book together I want to acknowledge the vital help I have received from my neighbours, family and friends. In particular I want to thank Tony Allen, Veronica and Tim Johnston, Lyulph Lubbock, 5th Lord Avebury and David Tedman for their patience, family archives and photographs. I am particularly indebted to the Chislehurst Society for access to their gallery of images known as the Ribbons Collection.

Whilst every effort has gone to trace copyright holders, many old images have been purchased from postcard collections and old library stocks. Several images are not ideally suited to reproduction in print but they are invaluable to the local story, so please appreciate them from the perspective of the pre digital era in which they were created.

I've enjoyed discovering these stories, I hope you do too. It was a somewhat indulgent journey of personal learning not an academic exercise for me, so you won't find footnotes or an index. However, if you find things along the way, please don't hesitate to continue the story and contact me. Joanna.friel@yahoo.co.uk

Joanna Friel
July 2018

Nathaniel Strode

1. The Camden Park Estate

1860 – 1890
Nathaniel Strode: Property Developer Extraordinaire

Lubbock Road forms the southern edge of the Camden Park Estate, acres of prime real estate named after illustrious Elizabethan antiquarian William Camden. The whole estate was purchased by Nathaniel Strode in July 1860, and a decade later the house, Camden Place, briefly became home to the exiled Napoleon III, former Emperor of the French.

No story of Lubbock Road is complete or can really even begin without understanding the legacy of Nathaniel William John Strode. Paternalistic benefactor, altruistic Francophile, or more likely a latter-day property developer with an eye for a profit. Strode's is the name found on all the conveyances of the original Lubbock Road properties. He parcelled up the building plots and quite deliberately 'designed' the development of his estate.

According to *The History of Chislehurst*, by E.A Webb,, G.W. Miller and J. Beckwith, 'Before 1875 the road only gave access to five villa residences built in what had been a small wood known as Raggles Wood'. In 1861, there were only four villas, with steady development by Strode into the 1870s. From a 1934 Kentish Times article, covering the 100th birthday of Octavia Freese (resident of Granite Lodge: more of her later), I learned that the road was once a gated cul-de-sac, just a muddy track known as New Road, with a footpath down to the quarry at the western end.

The chalk outcrop running roughly north-west to south-east between Elmstead and Chislehurst, gave rise to a local chalk mining industry spanning several centuries, the most visible evidence of which is the popular tourist attraction of Chislehurst Caves. However, an early example of chalk extraction in the area was discovered in May 1857, when a bottle-shaped cave was broken into by chalk miners excavating under Camden Park. The site was examined by 'a few gentlemen' and written up by Robert Booth Latter in the first volume of Archaeologia Cantiana, in which he concluded that it had been dug before the 5th century and was probably sunk to obtain marl for fertiliser. Roman pottery was discovered inside, and today remains of ancient electrical cable can be seen festooned around the galleries, possibly dating from 1872, when Nathanial Strode had the caves illuminated for a geologist's visit on 15 June that year.

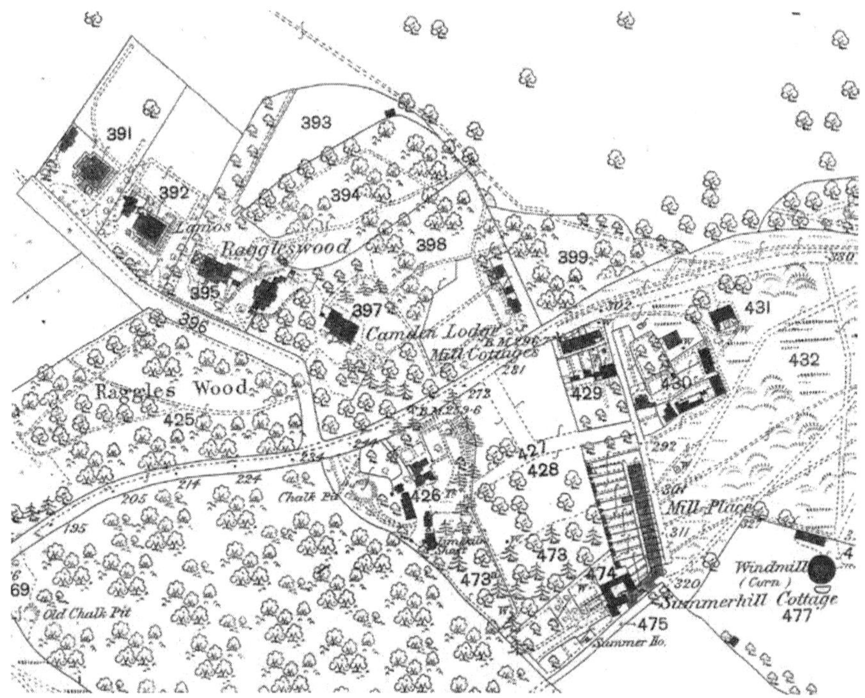

Map of 1862, showing the first part of what was to become Lubbock Road

According to sales indentures relating to the earliest properties in the road, development began from 1861. Strode clearly had designs on the type of 'estate' he intended to shape. He firmly stated in the documents that houses 'may be used as the professional residence of a duly qualified doctor, solicitor, dentist or other similar profession, making no show of business beyond one small brass plate'. I wonder if 'banker' fulfilled that criterion, or 'architect' or 'tea merchant'. These were the occupations of the first residents of the road.

I find it quite incredible that Strode's legacy does not remain in any place or street name in the area. The only obvious mark he has left behind is his coat of arms above the doorway of Camden Place and, rather discreetly, his name is marked on a brass plate at Christ Church.

For some time, although I had found out enough about his background to sketch a picture in my mind of what he was like, he remained something of an enigma, ever present but controlling our destiny from the shadows. But then I had one of my eureka moments, one that thrilled me and one that no one else, bar another local history buff, could really share, so you'll just have to come with me on this bit of the discovery and pretend to be as excited as I was!

On a rainy day, I was messing about on the internet and came across a 'Gravestone Photographic Resource' site. Just one of those morbid things that I do! Intrigued, I clicked 'S' on the alphabetical list, and Strode came up. This led me to the grave of one Alexander Ross Strode, buried in 1851. Also, on the headstone, with 'relationship unknown' was Nathaniel William John Strode, 1817–1889; this was my man! In requesting a photo of the headstone – it was in Greyfriars Cemetery in Edinburgh of all places, that of Greyfriars Bobby fame – one could leave a message about individual research interests.

Literally within the space of a day, an email popped into my inbox from Richard Strode, who turned out to be Nathaniel's great-great grandson. I had put in my message that I would love to see a picture of what Nathaniel looked like. There was an attachment to the email. My heart was pounding at this point. It was a picture of 'Nat', as his family refers to him. The whole of Lubbock Road probably heard my shouts of joy, but they would never have understood. Instead, the poor Chair of the Chislehurst Society, Tony Allen, with whom I had recently been swapping historical anecdotes, got the full force of my exultation over the phone! I'm sure he was expecting a deeper, more meaningful conversation about the minutes of a previous meeting or some such, but he just had to listen to a batty female going on about a long-dead character who was only a name to him. He did his best to register a level of interest that satisfied me, but it's been a difficult thrill to contain, as far as I am concerned.

Once I cooled off, I swapped information with Richard Strode, and we met that spring. His image of Nat was taken from a miniature painting which was secured in a small gold locket which had been in the Strode family for as long as Richard could remember. The image is resonant of a patriarch, a confident gentleman, and certainly to me seems to have a Napoleonic style about him. Nat's background is interesting; from my research, it appears that he was of Scottish descent, but the family always thought they were from Somerset (which makes sense, from the location of the town of Strode itself). *The History of Stirlingshire, Titled and Untitled Aristocracy* has him descended from Nathaniel Nugent Strode of Candie House, Muiravonside, Linlithgow. The family oral tradition marks them out as being from Somerset, but there certainly was a Scottish connection;

Camden Park Estate 1893

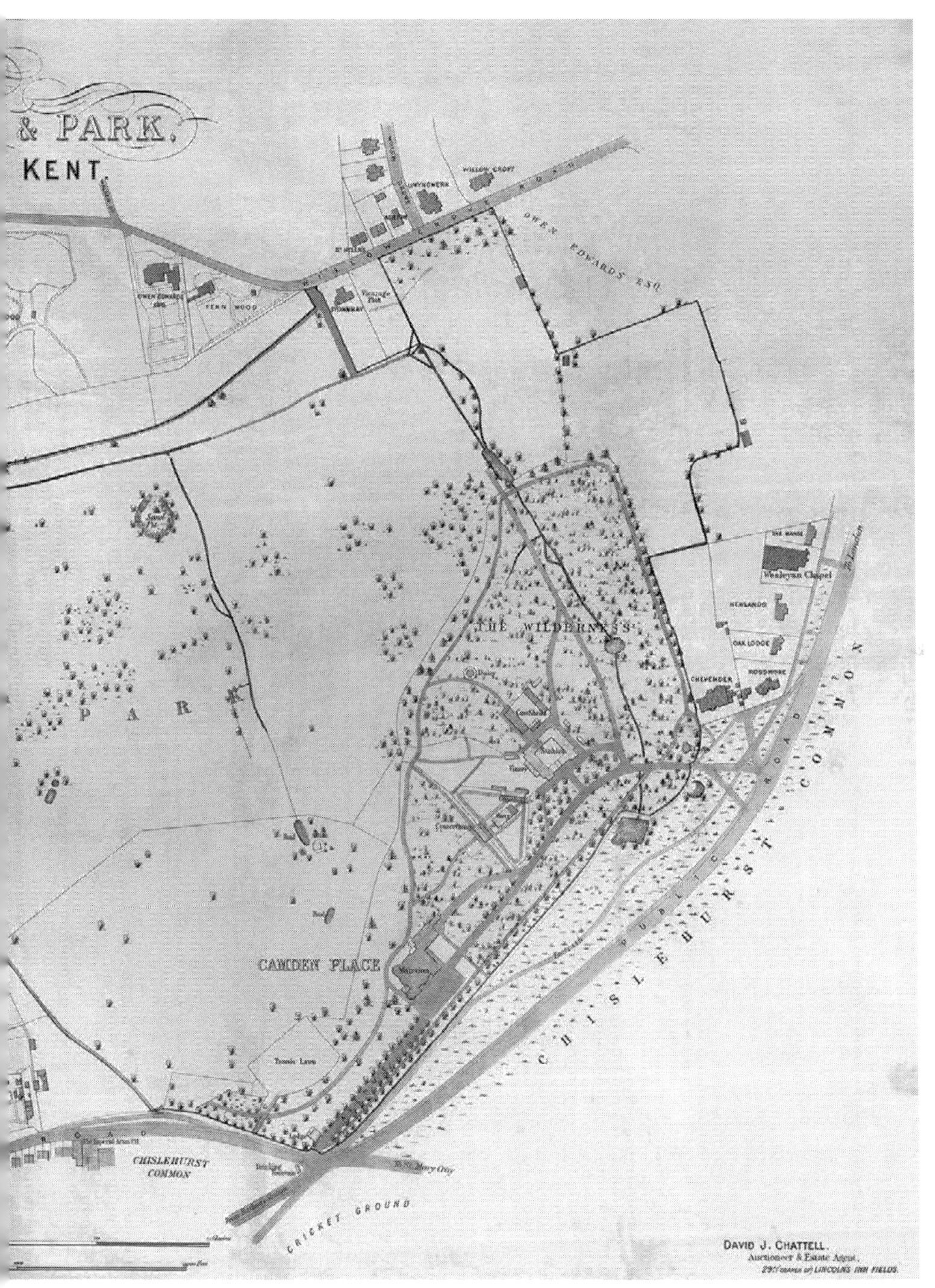
& PARK,
KENT.
WILLOW CROFT
OWEN EDWARDS ESQ.
FERN WOOD
THE WILDERNESS
Wesleyan Chapel
OAK LODGE
P A R K
CAMDEN PLACE
Tennis Lawn
CHISLEHURST COMMON
CHISLEHURST PUBLIC ROAD
CHISLEHURST COMMON
CRICKET GROUND
To London
DAVID J. CHATTELL.
Auctioneer & Estate Agent.

Richard's grandmother told a story of an ancestor losing his head for joining the wrong side in Scotland. Richard's grandfather was seen in pictures wearing natty Scottish attire, complete with kilt and cap. Richard bears the name Ross amongst his Christian names, so some Scottish resonance remains.

Candie House appears to have been a farm with a coal mine. It's hard to believe this provided Nathaniel's riches, but he obviously had the wherewithal to buy both the Camden Park Estate and a not insignificant mansion at Cranmore, as well as a property in The Albany, Piccadilly. He is listed in the *County Families of the United Kingdom*, but that was in 1861, following the purchase of Camden Park. Perhaps his mother was from moneyed stock: Caroline Kirk, the daughter of (this made me laugh) Captain Kirk.

Nathaniel Nugent Strode served as a British officer in the Sicilian Regiment of Foot (an offshoot of the British 16th Regiment), and married Nathaniel's mother in Gibraltar in 1812. Nathaniel was born at the Colchester Garrison in 1816 (a year's difference to the date on the gravestone!). He attended Dr Burney's School in Greenwich, a boarding school that produced many illustrious Victorians and was renowned for its education of well-heeled naval and military personnel. Nathaniel went on to train as a solicitor and worked for Fladgate & Co., a law partnership that still exists today.

Fladgate & Co. is significant in this unfolding story. The firm specialised in that era in trusteeship for the gentry, providing legitimate channels for the passing of funds to illegitimate children. During the first exile of Louis-Napoleon (later Napoleon III) in England, following the defeat of Napoleon Bonaparte at Waterloo, Louis had formed an attachment to a young English beauty, Emily Rowles, whose father owned Camden Place. Louis often visited her there in the 1830s. In 1846, he met another English girl, Elizabeth Ann Haryett, an aspiring actress, who had changed her name to Elizabeth Howard, and had had a son by a married man, Major Mountjoy Martyn. He bestowed a fortune on her, by way of estate in Piccadilly, when she passed the child off as that of her parents. This fortune was managed for her by way of a trust by her consummately discreet lawyer from Fladgate & Co., Nathaniel Strode, who, coincidentally, also lived in Piccadilly. Elizabeth made herself respectable by going through a nominal marriage ceremony with Clarence Trelawney. This ceremony took place at St James' Piccadilly, and the principal witness was none other than Nathaniel Strode.

Strode, too, may have felt the need for some respectable marriage, and in

1872 he married Eleanor Courtney at St James' Piccadilly. Eleanor, half his age, bore him three children, named familiarly Eugenie, Louis and, finally, possibly having run out of Imperial namesakes, Algernon Charles Ross, who was the great-grandfather of my contact, Richard. All three were baptised in the Parish of Chislehurst.

Nat describes himself in the 1861 census as 'a gentleman', but by 1881 he is a 'landowner'. He certainly had grand designs for his estate in Chislehurst. According to Webb's *History*, Strode allowed a sham fight to be staged between Bickley and the rising ground of Camden Place. The purpose of this was apparently to bring Chislehurst to more public notice as providing good sites for the building of houses for the gentry! Remember this was before the arrival of the railway. The first four houses were built on Strode's land in what became, five years later, Lubbock Road.

The Strode family returned to Camden Park when the Empress Eugénie left in 1881. However, Nat's tenure was not to last very much longer. He died at Bray Court near Maidenhead in Berkshire on 26 February 1889, but as we know he was buried in an ancestral plot in Scotland. His young widow married his land agent Frederick George Adcock, and it was as Mrs Adcock that she signed the sale indenture of Camden Park to William Willett in 1890.

Richard Strode and the plaque to Nathaniel Strode at Christ Church

John Lubbock

2. Lamas

1861 - 1865
John Lubbock: Modern Savages and Bank Holidays

The name John Lubbock may not immediately spring to mind as a local Chislehurst hero of the 19th century; however, we have a lot to be grateful to him for. As you walk or drive along Lubbock Road, it is here that the great man lived very happily with his first wife Ellen, and their young family, for just four years, from 1861. He has the distinction of being the MP who passed the Bank Holiday Act in 1871, and at that time he was lauded by the British people as 'Saint Lubbock'.

The Friel family moved into Lubbock Road in January 2000 with some great excitement as it meant, at last, that schools were within walking distance. I suspect that excitement was mostly on my part, as principal chauffeur, but still it was a great move. The house, number 68, though tired and much in need of updating, instantly became home, and I quickly learned how much sugar each builder took in his tea, while the children and animals got used to having skips on the drive. However, after far too many telephone calls from sales reps and delivery drivers asking where 'Loobock'

View of Lamas, c.1864, from Amy Lubbock's album

Road was, I did feel it was time to work out what that name really was all about.

Soon, I was drawn to a notice at High Elms in nearby Farnborough, advertising a free talk and display about the life and work of Lubbock, given by his great-grandson and family archivist, Lyulph Lubbock. My introduction to a whole new world had begun.

I learned that John's father was Sir John William Lubbock, a mathematician who deserves recognition today for tide timetables. I also learned of John's very special relationship with his near neighbour Charles Darwin, and much besides. John had left school, Eton, when he was 14 and had not experienced a university education, instead joining his father's bank, Lubbock, Forster & Co. He became an eminently successful banker, creating the cheque clearing system still in place today. Lubbock's wealth came from the family bank, which, in 1914, sold out to Coutts for £2 million.

John spent many spare hours (he was very hard-working and never, in fact, considered any hours to be 'spare') with Charles Darwin, just a couple of miles from High Elms. Darwin was 25 years Lubbock's senior but isolated at Downe House and subject to depression. Young Lubbock was the only person Darwin would tolerate around the place; his gift for natural history endeared him to his reclusive neighbour. The two would often be cloistered in Darwin's study and Darwin even gave John a very special telescope which can still be seen on display by English Heritage at Downe House. Under Darwin's tutelage, John became the youngest ever member of the Royal Society at the age of only 24. Lubbock had discovered the skeletal remains of a Musk Ox at Maidenhead in 1855 with Charles Kingsley (author of the Water Babies), and the fossilised bones of a Mammoth Ox in a gravel pit at Green Street Green. His collection is in the British Museum to this day.

It is believed that John can be credited with making some of the drawings for Darwin's On the Origin of Species. John had very fine draughtsman's skills and never wore glasses. He corrected errors in the mathematics and was subject to Darwin's critical onslaught but was said by Darwin to be 'one of only two or three supporters I can count on'.

John married Ellen Hordern, 'Nellie', a distant cousin, in 1856. The new family, with three children, Amy, John and Constance, lived with John's parents and his eleven younger siblings at High Elms. I can quite understand Ellen's need for a home of her own!

John Lubbock was already familiar with Chislehurst when the family arrived in 1861: aware of the Roman archaeological finds in the quarry;

certainly a visitor to Chislehurst Caves, where he had etched his name in a smoky section of chalk and found horseshoe bats; he was also a regular demon bowler and left-handed batsman for West Kent Cricket Club on the Common at the top of Old Hill. John was a cricket lover, for some years acting as secretary to the club; he was good friends with Philip Norman who wrote the club's annals. John used to practice in Chislehurst every Saturday and used the train connection to his London bank from Bickley, then known as Southborough, during the week.

The family moved into a substantial detached house called Lamas, named after the family seat in North Norfolk. The hamlet of Lammas is not too far from Cromer, and if you ever visit that part of the world you will find a memorial to Anna Sewell, author of Black Beauty, there too! Lamas (I have failed to establish why the second m was never utilised), the Chislehurst house, stood where 103 -105A Lubbock Road stands today, behind four brick gateposts – now reduced to two. The Lubbocks did a lot of entertaining. A friend wrote 'We used to go to Lamas on Sunday afternoons and sit on the long flight of steps having delightful talks with all the rising scientific men of the day'. Imagine the scene, described by Ellen in her correspondence with Charles Darwin: sitting on the steps facing the sunset, with no church spire of St George's, Bickley (built in 1865), no church bells pealing from Christ Church (1872), and no houses opposite (where Sandy Ridge and the Vicarage now stand). Chislehurst made an excellent place to set up home.

Two more children were born at Lamas, Norman and Gertrude, born in December 1861 and February 1863, respectively.

The Darwin Correspondence Project confirmed to me the most distinctive visitor, who really puts Lubbock Road on the historic map. Ellen wrote a letter in the New Year of 1862 to Emma Darwin asking if 'Mr Darwin could be persuaded to come here next Sunday either to early dinner at quarter before one o'clock – or to stay all night. He would see nobody but John, not even me; most likely, for I am not quite strong yet [following the birth of Norman] and I will take care his bed is aired. John doesn't know I am writing this, but I have heard him lately so often wish if he could only have a talk with Mr Darwin and I know he can't manage to get over to Downe now as he used to from High Elms – so I thought I would just try what I could to persuade Mr Darwin to come here'. Ellen's persuasion must have worked. Charles Darwin came to lunch at Lamas on the 15 February 1862; this evidence is confirmed by a letter from Darwin himself to J.B. Innes on 24 February: 'We went a few days ago to lunch with the John Lubbocks and they evidently seem thoroughly to enjoy their new home and surroundings.' Result!

John and his wife entertained many scientists fiercely enamoured of Darwin's theories of natural selection, known as the X Club. These were Thomas Huxley (a biologist specialising in anatomy, known as 'Darwin's Bulldog'), George Busk (a naval surgeon, zoologist and palaeontologist), Edward Frankland (a chemist, one of the discoverers of helium), Joseph Hooker (founder of geographical botany and Darwin's closest friend), Herbert Spencer (philosopher, biologist and anthropologist and prominent liberal political theorist of the time), William Spottiswoode (mathematician and physicist, president of the Royal Society) and John Tyndall (an Irish physicist making discoveries in infrared radiation).

Herbert Spencer gives us an insight into life at Lamas in his autobiography. In 1862, he described a day with John Lubbock: various activities before breakfast, rapid glance at The Times on the way to the station, reading some pages from a book he carried, banking in the morning, political business or scientific society after dinner. Spencer was astonished at Lubbock's 'versatility' and his wife's 'vivacity'.

Quite how much John was home to enjoy life in Chislehurst is debatable. In researching his first book, he made five journeys to the Continent and Scotland between 1861 and 1864. The result of this research was that Lubbock Road was actually named in 1865 in honour of the publication of his seminal and popular book, *Prehistoric Times: as illustrated by Ancient Remains and the Manner and Customs of Modern Savages*, first published from Lamas. This eminent work became a best seller around the world.

Lubbock was the first scientist to coin the terms palaeolithic, mesolithic and neolithic. Many of his archaeological finds came from travels overseas, Denmark in particular. Considering his lack of early education, Lubbock was clearly a very able man, a polyglot, fluent in eight different languages, enabling him to converse with scientists internationally.

Darwin congratulated Lubbock on his book in June 1865: 'The latter half of your book has been read aloud to me and the style was so clear and easy (we both think it perfection) that I am now going back to the beginning...It has quite delighted me for now the public will know what kind of man you are which I am proud to think I discerned a dozen years ago'.

I ventured to ask Lyulph what he knew about the road in Chislehurst named after his great-grandfather, but other than confirming that he had

A drawing of John Lubbock at the time he lived at Lamas

Ellen Lubbock

definitely lived there, I learned no more from him – at this stage.

One of the better cups of coffee I enjoyed on this research journey was with my immediate neighbour at Sandy Ridge, Viv Smith. Viv knew of my interest in history and really inspired me with the gift of a book, *Home*, by Julie Myerson (a must-read if you are researching the history of your house; even wallpaper can be a lead!). Viv invited me to coffee with the former owners of her house, which led to my seeing title deeds and learning so much more about land transactions involving Lubbock, Lamas, bankers, Sandy Ridge and my own home, originally called The Rookery. The former owner of Sandy Ridge happened to be Bruce Hurn, a recently retired committee member of the Chislehurst Society. Unbeknownst to me, he contacted the Society chairman and I subsequently received an interesting invitation to come along to a meeting. I was even foolish enough to offer to give a talk to the members of the Chislehurst Society on my Lubbock discoveries. The talk must have been advertised more widely than I had anticipated: imagine my disquiet when I saw Lyulph Lubbock and his wife enter the room and sit in the audience; how could I possibly tell them anything they didn't already know?

However, thanks to the title deeds from Bruce, and a Chislehurst Society photograph that Tony Allen had shared with me, I was able to show the Lamas landscape. Unbelievably, that led to Lyulph being able to identify a previously unknown house (c. 1864) in Amy Lubbock's photograph album as Lamas. A whole new and much closer vista of Lubbock's time in 'our' road emerged.

The Lubbocks were academic liberals, united by 'a devotion to science, pure and free, untrammelled by religious dogma', wrote his biographer, Horace Hutchinson. Perhaps it's just as well that they left the road before the church was built! On the death of his father in July 1865, Sir John, as he then became, left Lamas and returned to the family seat at High Elms.

Sir John became an MP for Maidstone in 1870, and his long political career with the Liberal party began. He was a founder member of the Electoral Reform Society. Whenever you visit an ancient monument, walk in open spaces, visit a public library or write a cheque, be grateful to Sir John Lubbock, for he passed the Acts of Parliament that enabled these institutions to thrive. But most of all, you should recall Sir John when you enjoy a day with your family away from work on a Bank Holiday. As a banker himself, he wanted his staff to enjoy some hard-earned days of 'repose and recreation', but he had always intended Bank Holidays to be universal in their appeal, not simply for bank employees. Initially, his bill was called The National Holidays Act, but as a Bank Holiday Act it attracted less parliamentary attention and received swift passage through the House of Commons. No one could have anticipated the scenes that would be witnessed at Cannon Street and Charing Cross stations as a result, as thousands of people queued for space on trains and steamers to Ramsgate and Margate. The days were so much appreciated that initially they were known as 'St Lubbock's Days'. Given the bad press towards banks of late, there has been a call in Parliament to return to this soubriquet!

In 1873, Sir John was one of the dignitaries who went to Camden Place to pay their respects to the late Emperor, Napoleon III.

Ellen died in 1879, and Sir John went on to marry Alice Fox Pitt in 1884. John and Alice had five children together, Ursula, Irene, Harold, Eric and Maurice. Lyulph is descended from Maurice Lubbock. Sir John continued his scientific interests, keeping a pet wasp and training his pet dog to read! He published another best seller, *Ants, Wasps and Bees* in 1882. (One of his brothers, Frederick, lived at what is now the National Trust house and gardens, Emmetts. Emmett is another name for an ant!)

The year 1882 also bore witness to the death of Charles Darwin. He is buried in Westminster Abbey. Lubbock was one of nine pall bearers, along with Spottiswoode, Hooker and Huxley from Chislehurst X Club days, and Alfred Wallace, another supporter of natural selection.

In 1888, Lubbock was made president of the London Chamber of Commerce and became a Privy Councillor in 1890. A peerage was conferred on him on Christmas Day 1899; he took the name Lord Avebury after the stone circle in Wiltshire which he had brought in order to protect it from builders! In May 1908, he went before the House of Commons to give evidence in support of another Chislehurst resident, William Willett, and his Daylight Saving Bill.

Overall, it would be hard to name anyone 'who did more useful things, in more fields and yet won less lasting fame for it', as Bill Bryson commented in his book *The History of Almost Everything*. Lord Avebury died on 28 May 1913, and his name rather disappeared along with that pre-War era. He is buried in the woods near St Giles Church, Farnborough, Kent, and his memorial cross in the churchyard is a thing of beauty, cleverly depicting his lifetime interests: a stone circle, Bronze Age axes and a bee skep.

His legacy continued in the Liberal parliamentary family of Eric Lubbock (he who won the famous Orpington by-election in 1962), and in

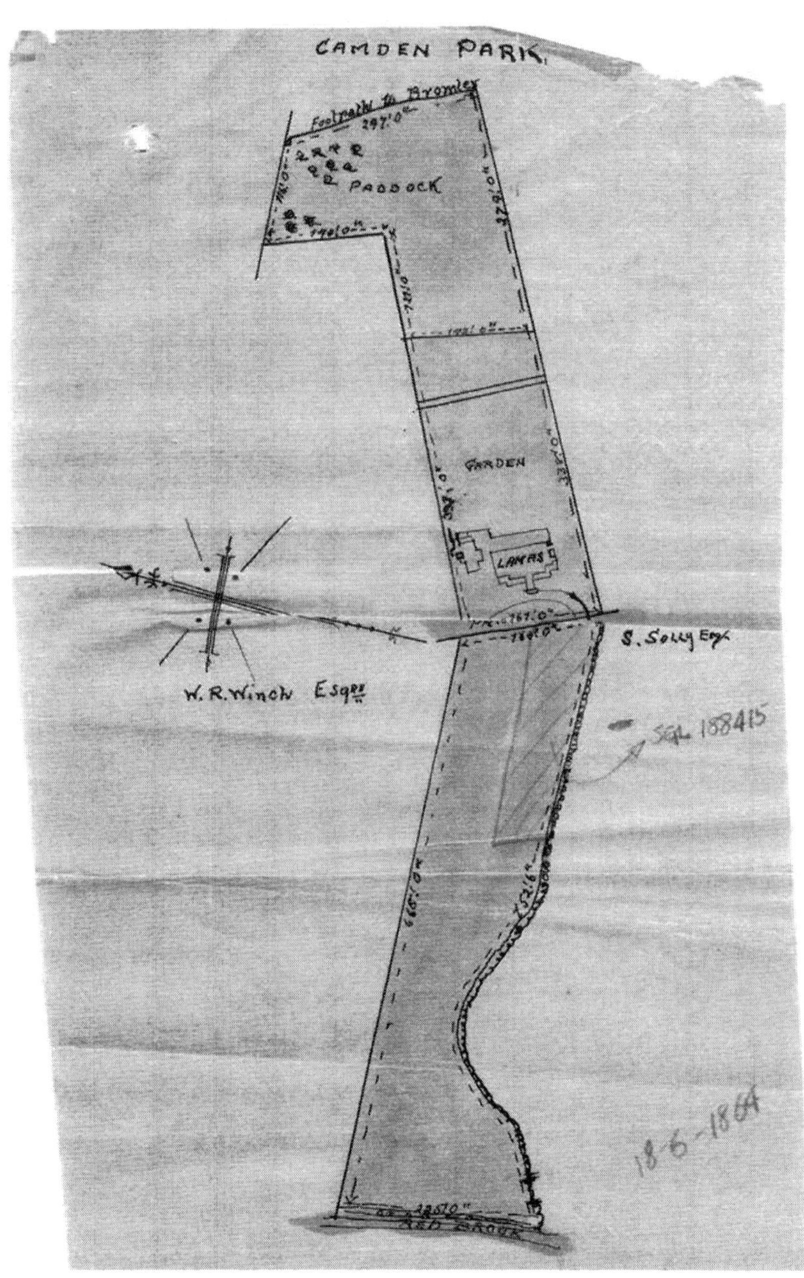

Land conveyance for Lamas 1861

the wonderful BEECHE Centre at High Elms. The family mansion on that site no longer stands. It burned to the ground in 1967, and guess which day that occurred - yes, August Bank Holiday! The very significant heritage of Sir John, his work in relation to archaeology and civic responsibility, can be seen locally in the Lubbock Gallery at Bromley Historic Collections. His name can often be seen on foundation stones of public libraries, for the passing of the Public Libraries Act, ensuring a library in every major town, was one of his legacies.

Residents of Lubbock Road marked the centenary of the death of Sir John Lubbock in 2013 with the late Lord Avebury coming to unveil a Chislehurst Society plaque on the remaining gateposts at Lamas. We enjoyed a cake in the shape of 100 and played a great game of 'Guess the Act', recalling all 30 of his Acts of Parliament, passed for the benefit of our nation, not least, of course, the 1871 Bank Holiday Act!

1867 - 1895
Francis Johnston: Coffee and Cricket

When I learned that Sir John Lubbock had left Lamas after only four years, in 1865, I kept looking out of my window and wondering what had become of that substantial house in the wake of his departure. I knew from an old photograph that the place became St Hugh's Prep School in 1909, but what of the intervening forty years? Not one to let such a question go, I embarked on what became a very fruitful search for the residents of Lamas, a delightful correspondence with a seriously organised and professionally trained archivist and, most particularly, an hilarious trip to Paris to see a picture which reduced me to tears, a picture which was destined to be the cover of this book.

The 1871 census was my first port of call. This revealed the name Francis Johnston, aged 40, his wife Caroline and five children; the third, a daughter, Caroline after her mother, was the first child born in Chislehurst in autumn 1867. I subsequently discovered that both Sir John Lubbock and Francis Johnston were members of the Folklore Society; in fact, Sir John was the vice president. This conjured up a wonderful image of the two gentlemen negotiating the sale and purchase of Lamas on a handshake at an evening meeting of the society: dinner, cigars, maybe a conversation about cricket over coffee (more of that later) and a swift signing of the paperwork, job done, Howzat!

Francis was also a member of the Statistical Society, of which Sir John was president; I have little doubt that the two would have met there as well.

Once into a census, one naturally goes on to 1881 and beyond. I was not disappointed, and found the family continuing in residence in 1891. The census revealed the names of nine children in total. Obviously I continued my census search right through to 1911, which was fortunate. Francis lived until July of that year, and the 1911 census reveals so much more than earlier records. In the column for children alive, only seven appear, with three listed as deceased. So that equalled 10 children in total and I only knew about eight of them. I did know of an early death of one child, Bertram the eldest, so that left me with two unknown children, and my curiosity was sparked.

I was beginning to get sucked in to this man's life and his family and was itching to know more. I struck gold via the 1881 census. The eldest child, Bertram, was written on the Ancestry.com transcription as 'Bestraw', clearly an error, which I was delighted to see another family researcher had corrected. I ventured, via the message system in Ancestry, to contact the author of that correction. This turned out to be the wonderful Veronica Johnston, with whom I exchanged many informative e-mails. The journey had begun.

Francis Johnston was the third son of Edward Johnston and Harriet Moke. His father had founded E. Johnston & Co. Ltd, coffee traders. Even that titbit entertained me, as next door to Lamas lived W.R.Winch, a gentleman who made his fortune in the tea trade.

Francis was involved with the family coffee business until he retired owing to ill health, in 1866. He became one of the founders, and the first chairman, of the London Produce Clearing House, and was a well known figure in the City. He became a director of the London Joint Stock Bank, later the Midland Bank, so he would certainly have been a banking contemporary of Sir John Lubbock.

Francis had married Caroline Earle, daughter of Sir Hardman Earle, at All Saints Parish Church in Liverpool in July 1856. Tragedy befell the Johnstons early on. I learned from Veronica about the first-born daughters of the couple, Beatrice Mary, born in 1857, and Margaret, born in 1859. However I was struck by the closeness of dates in the deaths of these two little girls, Beatrice in November 1859 and her little sister Margaret a month earlier in October 1859. Not one to let this little mystery go un-investigated, I ordered the death certificates from the General Register Office. Margaret was only 19 days old when she died of diphtheria at the family home in

Wavertree, Liverpool. Francis was in attendance at her death. In their grief, and possibly to escape the dark October skies of Merseyside, Francis and Caroline and their two year old daughter Beatrice travelled to the balmier climes of Torquay. However, poor Francis was again present at the death of his offspring; three weeks after the death of her sister, Beatrice succumbed to the ravages of croup after fighting an infection for three days. The real heartache behind this story is that croup was in those days primarily due to the presence of diphtheria, so Beatrice was very probably doomed by the incubating infection of her baby sister. These days, this childhood infection would be treated with a dose of antibiotics, but in Victorian England this childhood death was all too common. Poor Caroline, she had only just given birth a month before, and was now grieving for both her children.

Back home at Sandford Lodge, Wavertree, in 1861, Caroline gave birth to Bertram. Caroline went on to produce seven more children. A child born almost every other year: two more boys, Alexander and Horace James, and five daughters, Caroline, Violet, Harriet Monica, Mildred and Vera. Vera was born in Chelsea, indicating the possibility of an additional London home for the Johnstons. Born in the first months of 1874, Vera would never know her mother, who was to die in December of the following year, leaving Francis with a young brood ranging in age from 14 years to 18 months. Hardy surprising, then, that in the 1881 census Francis is described as 'retired', and Lamas is run by a cook/housekeeper, a butler, a housemaid, a kitchen maid, head nurse, nursery maid and a groom.

Caroline was buried at St Nicholas but her death certificate tells of further sadness for the family. Francis was at her side when she died; she was only 43, but her condition had been diagnosed for several years. She had Melasma Addisonii, which is a facial pigmentation associated with liver disease, and it is so often seen in women during pregnancy that it became known as the mask of pregnancy; it must have been very disfiguring. I can't help but feel sorry for Caroline. All those babies, the deaths of her two little girls, and she herself was very likely hidden away from social intercourse for much of her short life.

However if she hadn't had all those children, I might never have had my quirky visit to Paris to see a portrait of them – the cover picture of this book! Whilst searching on the web, I came across a portrait for auction at Christie's entitled 'The Johnston Children'. I was so excited to find this, and contacted Veronica immediately, with various questions as to the almost certain errors in the auction catalogue relating to the picture. The portrait

Francis and Caroline Johnston c.1856

Francis Johnston

Caroline Johnston

was commissioned in 1877 of five of the Johnston children. Veronica and the family had no knowledge as to where the portrait was set. The catalogue stated that the portrait was commissioned by Edward Johnston and the children are depicted in the grounds of his house in Sidmouth, Devon! I had to set the record straight and indeed see the portrait for myself.

Edward Johnston had died in 1876, so it is impossible that he commissioned a portrait a year after his demise. Francis was living at Chislehurst in 1877 and owned Sidmouth after 1901. The children in the portrait are Alex, Horace James (known as 'Jim'), Caroline 'Madge', Monica and Mildred, the children of Francis and Caroline. The portrait details the slopes of a garden with mature trees, a house with prominent chimneys in the background and a distant church spire off to the west. Lamas was built on a slope within the mature acreage of Camden Park. Lamas had distinctive chimneys according to my aerial photograph; and Christ Church to the west was originally built with a spire, its tower only built in 1879. The oil on canvas is described by Christie's as 'a highly realised portrait, the Victorian attention to detail alleviated with just a hint of Belle Epoque swagger, an impressive testament to the skill of this little-known painter [Robert Antoine Muller]'. I suspect Bertram is not in the picture as he was away at school; the boys were educated by Mr Meyrick Jones at Yverdon House, Blackheath, and then privately at Heidelberg and Paris. Bertram would have been 16 in 1877, and very likely a boarder overseas.

Veronica gave me the excellent news (for me) that the portrait had failed to reach its commission price and was still in the family possession, being with the grandson of Jim, hanging in his apartment in Paris. Fortuitously my e-mails had been copied to Tim, the current owner, and I received an open invitation to come and visit! Well, not being one to let a bit of English Channel come between me and a slice of road history, I headed to Paris. It was December and grey and damp, but fortified by the knowledge that Tim owned a wine bar, I made my way to the slopes of Montmartre to step back into a Victorian family that I felt I knew personally!

The portrait is beautiful, huge by anyone's standards, covering the whole wall of Tim's apartment. There before me were those poor, motherless children surrounded by the ephemera of a Victorian childhood: cricket bat and ball, a hoop and a stick, a picnic basket, reading book and a wee Highland terrier on Madge's knee. The girls are neat in their pastel-coloured frocks, and the boys are wearing matching neckties and pocket handkerchiefs. Lamas is in the background, nestled beside many of the pine trees that dominate our skyline even today, and with a smoking chimney, presumably warming the nursery for Violet and Vera indoors.

But children grow up and families move on. Madge was the first to marry, on Tuesday, 17 August 1888. She was 21. She married Richard Heywood Jones of Badsworth Hall, Yorkshire. His family were related to the Earles, so a match may have been inevitable. The Bromley Record describes it as a 'fashionable wedding' conducted by the Rev. W. St Aubyn, uncle of the bride, and by Canon Murray of Chislehurst. The bride was given away by her father and had seven bridesmaids: her sisters, as well as Miss Tiarks from Foxbury, a cousin, and a friend. There were 100 guests at the wedding breakfast and there was a grand ball given in the evening. The wedding presents were 'a splendid and costly collection' and the honeymoon was spent in a shooting box in Aberdeenshire!

Sadness engulfed the family only a couple of years later. Bertram died on 5 July 1890 of yellow fever in Rio de Janeiro, where he was working for the family business. He is buried in Gamboa Cemetery in that city. One wonders when his father and siblings last saw him, at Madge's wedding perhaps; he is certainly listed on the marriage certificate as being present.

There were two weddings in 1893, one in London and one in France. The first was Alex to Audrey Alers Hankey, whose family lived on Widmore Road, Bromley. The second marriage of 1893 was indeed a second marriage. Aged 61, Francis re-married, a Canadian woman, eleven years his junior, Emma Sterling. The wedding took place in Hyres in the south of France in April.

The Johnstons moved from Lamas in the mid 1890s. The house was sold to Mr Robert Hunter, a merchant trading in goods from Morocco. One wonders whether Francis knew him via his own commercial trading.

It was the date of Harriet's wedding in June 1896 that gave me the first indication of the move from Chislehurst. Her marriage certificate lists her residence as Dunsdale, Westerham. She married Sir Charles Wyndham of the Bengal Cavalry, and the service at the parish church of Westerham was conducted by none other than Canon Murray.

Then there is the distinguished story of Horace James. Jim became a soldier, a Lieutenant Colonel in the Duke of Wellington's Regiment, and was awarded the Distinguished Service Order in 1902 in recognition of services in South Africa at the Orange River and Cape Colony. He married Florence Hope Brown-Clayton, daughter of Irishman, William Brown-Clayton, on 28 April 1904. They had three children, Francis William born

Francis John Johnston (1831-1911)
by Mark Millbank c.1900

in 1905, Patrick James in 1908, and Hope Caroline. It is from the eldest son, Francis William, that Tim comes into the family and inherited the portrait in question.

Jim saw active service in the First World War and, poignantly, it is from his war record that I know he called his marital home in Peek Crescent, Wimbledon, 'Lamas'. He must have had some happy associations with his Chislehurst childhood home to remember it thus. But that war record does not have a happy ending. Emma, his stepmother, posted a message in The Times on 26 August 1915, that her 'son' was reported missing in the Dardanelles between August 7 and 11. Jim had in fact been caught up in the Gallipoli disaster; he was the commanding officer and was taken prisoner, but was badly wounded. He was finally reported Killed in Action on 7 August 1915. He is remembered on the war memorial at Badsworth, where he had spent much of his time during training at his sister's, she having been widowed in 1900 when Richard was 'struck by lightning' whilst at camp with the local militia.

My Parisian host commented that the 1900 Mark Millbank image of Francis, which hung over the sideboard in the dining room of his father's home (reproduced on page 25), looked grumpy and disagreeable. It is certainly a somewhat serious portrayal, but when you think Francis suffered the early bereavements of his young daughters, the illness of his first wife and the loss of his eldest son far from home, it is not altogether surprising. I recall that Francis had retired due to 'ill health'; the 1911 census has him living in Sidmouth, Devon. He died that year on 29 July. His cause of death was Locomotor Ataxy, an inability to control one's own bodily movements.

Francis is buried in St Nicholas churchyard alongside Caroline. Emma died in Honiton in 1920. But what of that cricket connection I mentioned in my introduction? It transpires that Brian 'Johnners' Johnston is part of this clan. He was a grandson of Francis's brother, Reginald Eden Johnston, one-time Governor of the Bank of England. In 1922, Brian's father was drowned off a beach near Bude. Brian was only ten and subsequently was raised by his relatives. He joined the Johnston coffee empire but admitted he had no liking for the work. In 1938, he travelled to Santos in Brazil for eighteen months, but was struck down by an acute neurological condition. He resigned to join the army for the war and then joined the BBC in 1946, where he carved out his famous cricket commentary career. How Sir John Lubbock would have approved of that connection!

3. Raggleswood

1861-1937
Writer's Cramp, a Drinking Fountain and a Thousand Ships

Raggleswood had a succession of families living there from 1861 to 1937, and I have found close associations with St Nicholas Church, a brief link to the Walnuts shopping centre in Orpington, and even a baronetcy! The house is long gone but I looked at the original site, directly opposite my study window, as I wrote.

Raggles Wood is one of the Chislehurst woods that has now vanished. Dorothea Gibson (an amateur historian herself and resident of Camden Hill, Lubbock Road), wrote in Webb's *History* in 1899 that the derivation of the name Raggles Wood may be from the Anglo-Saxon word 'raggie' meaning rough, shaggy.

From an original indenture, I understand the first resident of the house named after that wood was Samuel Solly Esq., who is listed in an 1862 Kelly's Directory at this address. Mr Solly was a distinguished surgeon at St Thomas' Hospital. He was the son of a wealthy merchant and grew up at 5 Jeffrey's Square, St Mary Axe – a site now underneath 'The Gherkin'. Mr Solly lectured on anatomy and physiology, having completed his medical studies in Paris. According to his obituary, he was a skilful operator, a florid

An aerial photograph of Raggleswood

lecturer and a good clinical teacher; his opinion was specially sought in cases of injuries to the head and diseases of the joints, and he was the first doctor to use the term 'scriveners' palsy' – writer's cramp. He was an accomplished amateur artist; many of his lectures were personally illustrated, and his watercolours were displayed at the Royal Academy.

Solly had 11 children; the 15-roomed house of Raggleswood would certainly have accommodated them. He is variously listed as living in St Helen's Place, Bishopsgate, and Savile Row; Raggleswood was the country residence of the family. Webb's *History* refers to a brass plate beneath a southeast window in St Nicholas' Church dedicated to the memory of Lieutenant William Herbert Solly, 1859, Francis D Solly, 1862 and Charles Edmund Solly, 1860. These are three of Samuel and Jane Solly's sons. Charles died in 1840 at only four months old, of influenza. William was their second son, dying aged 24 in Cawnpore, India, and Francis Drake Solly was their fourth son, who died in Shanghai in 1862. He was a silk inspector. It is possible, though unproven, that he was working for the Courtauld family, as his older brother Lewis married Susan Courtauld in 1864. A family that suffered these cumulative tragedies could very well have wanted a permanent memorial at their place of worship. Sadly, the plaque and windows are no longer in place due to Second World War bomb blasts.

Two other sons went on to establish themselves with great repute in science. Samuel Edwin established a sanatorium in Colorado Springs for tuberculosis sufferers, being a sufferer himself. His obituary makes edifying reading, concluding with the words 'we all loved Solly'! Richard Harrison Solly, sixth son, was a recognised mineralogist and crystallographer working at the British Museum and the University of Cambridge, where, incidentally, he lodged next door to Marie Stopes! The youngest son, Henry Ernest, remained in Chislehurst, living at Sunnyways, now a dental practice on Prince Imperial Road. He, too, is buried in the churchyard of St Nicholas.

Samuel Solly moved to Folkstone in 1871, and died suddenly on 24 September, aged 66, at his London Savile Row residence. Mrs Jane Solly moved back to Chislehurst and died at Church Row in June 1889. She was one of the subscribers to the fund for the memorial to the Prince Imperial. Samuel and his wife are both buried in the churchyard. There is a marble bust to Samuel in the central hall at St Thomas' (as you might imagine, I had a good day out tracking that down), and the Solly prize and medal in the medical school were established with the proceeds of public subscriptions to his memory.

The Charles Janson fountain on Church Row, 1887

Detail from the Charles Janson fountain

The entrance to Raggleswood c.1890

The Janson family were in residence at Raggleswood at the time of the 1871 census; Eliza Janson was widowed in 1868 but brought at least five of her eleven children to Chislehurst. The Jansons were originally a Quaker family from North London. William Janson had been an underwriter with Lloyd's, as well as a property developer in Tottenham, where Jansons Road was constructed in 1863. Mr Janson also built a terrace of houses named after Harriett Beecher Stowe as he admired her work. Stowe Place still exists, in the London Borough of Haringey.

The connection with St Nicholas is the granite drinking fountain on the corner of the churchyard, dedicated to Rev. Charles Janson. He was the youngest of William and Eliza's children, dying aged 32 in 1884, as a missionary at Lake Nyassa, Malawi. His mother predeceased him by one year, aged 74. The Universities' Mission to Central Africa was founded in 1857 in response to a plea by the inspirational missionary and explorer David Livingstone. Charles Janson went to Oxford University and was part of the mission originated by Bishop Charles Mackenzie to set up an Anglican base at Lake Nyassa. The History of the Universities' Mission describes how Charles's last journals show him appreciating glowing hills, wooded vales and a hippopotamus taking an early bath. On 9 February 1884, Bishop Edward Steere, accompanied by Charles, reached a beach on the edge of the lake, seemingly the desired goal of the Mission for many years. They said it reminded them of the Sea of Galilee. Unfortunately, the rainy season had made their journey a very trying one and towards its close, Charles suffered from dysentery. 'Our brother fell asleep on Shrove Tuesday at Noon. If we had chosen one of our number' said Bishop Steere four months later 'of whom we should have said was fit for the kingdom of heaven, we should have chosen no one more clearly than Charles Janson'. He is buried by the lake under a cairn of stones. A steamer was named in his honour and launched on 6 September 1885 by Bishop Smithies. The vessel arrived safely in Likoma (an island on the lake on which a large Anglican Cathedral was later built, in 1911) on 22 January 1886, apparently fulfilling a much-desired dream of Bishop Mackenzie for a 'University boat'.

Charles's older sister Ellen is often mentioned in *The Bromley Record*. She obviously ran the Raggleswood household, hiring servants and providing references for tutors. According to Webb's *History*, she gifted the cross on the St Nicholas altar, it having been originally fixed to the altar book of her late brother. It was taken from the ruins of a fire at Matope and brought back to Chislehurst.

The family were not unused to tragedy, having lost a second son at sea off Alexandria in 1863, aged 21. There is a tribute to him on the family grave. Another son, Dearman Janson, (whose Christian name was his mother's maiden name) moved to a house, Northfield, now the site of Northfield Close at the top of Logs Hill, but at that time known as part of Elmstead Lane. He died in 1907 in a 'sanatorium for the insane' in Holloway, and is buried with his mother at St Nicholas.

By 1909, Kelly's Directory is showing another change of ownership, this time to William and Mary Vinson. They only had two children, but the 1911 census clearly states a house of 15 rooms. The Vinsons were a local farming family; William was born on his father Edward's farm in Halfway Street, Sidcup. In 1901, William and Mary were living in Orpington in a house called The Walnuts. Could this have been on the site of the current shopping centre? Think also of Vinson Court off Hurst Road in Sidcup and Vinson Close in Orpington. The Vinson fruit farming business still thrives in Kent.

The last resident, before Raggleswood was demolished, took the title of his baronetcy from the house. Sir Joseph William Isherwood took up residence in 1913 and was created Baron Raggleswood in the 1921 Birthday Honours list. The title became extinct on the death of his son without issue. He was a naval architect and invented the longitudinal construction of ships, known as the Isherwood system. He decided it was better to build a ship on its backbone rather than on its ribs and his system became so successful that more than 1,000 vessels had been built that way by the time of his death. During the First World War, Isherwood gave his designs for torpedo-proof cargo vessels to the government, free of charge. Described in his obituary as modest and retiring, a man of many friends and a great host, he was also Captain of the West Kent Golf Club in 1935. He died in 1937.

The name lives on in Raggleswood, a private road off Old Hill, part of which would have been within the grounds of the original house. Sir Joseph's widow moved to a new home in Logs Hill Close which she named Raggleswood House.

The aerial photograph, taken of the first houses in Lubbock Road, marks the end of an era. It was taken just ahead of the demolition of Raggleswood following Sir Joseph's death, coinciding with the end of the long lease on the land. The owner of one of the existing houses on the site says her father found many shards of coloured glass in the ground; were these from windows and elegant light fixtures that witnessed the comings and goings of Victorian family life?

Joseph Isherwood, Baron Raggleswood

4. Oakbank

1862-1886
Frederick Halsey Janson: Parochial Stalwart

One of the first residents in the road with an acceptable profession to Strode was solicitor, Frederick Halsey Janson, who arrived here in 1862. Frederick had been born in 1813 and lived to celebrate his 100th birthday. Married to Elizabeth Anne Tozer, he purchased one of the first four villas in the new road. The house was to become 'Oakbank' but on the earliest map, the house is named as 'Camden Lodge'. Frederick and Elizabeth had seven children when they came to Chislehurst and a further three were born here, the first being Florence in November 1862.

The couple had come from the Clapton area of London (then a semi-rural village), having been married at the new Friends' Meeting House in Paradise Fields, Hackney, in 1847: sounds like an auspicious start to a relationship! FHJ (as all solicitors were known by their initials) was articled to the then well-known firm of Messrs Smith & Bayley. On qualification in 1835, he became a partner. Following the death of Mr Bayley in 1852, FHJ became the sole surviving partner, but soon formed the firm of Janson, Cobb & Pearson. Aside from the law, FHJ had an interest in mathcmatics, and was a Fellow of the Statistical Society, of which his neighbour, Francis

A rather blurry aerial photograph of Oakbank

Johnston, was a member, and Sir John Lubbock was president. He also took an interest in taxonomy, the science of classification of organism groups. This led to his being elected a fellow of the Linnaean Society, to which he remained actively connected; indeed, he was its oldest fellow at the time of his death. Polymath Sir John Lubbock was also president of the Linnaean Society from 1881-86; the two men would have had distinct common ground.

In 1859, FHJ was appointed a deputy lieutenant of what was described then as 'The Tower Hamlets'. He was vice president of the London Institution and three times master of the Worshipful Company of Leathersellers. Adding to these titles, he was elected to the Council of the Incorporated Law Society in 1861. His London address was Westbourne Terrace, Hyde Park, and he was a member of both City and Constitutional clubs.

His growing family needed more commodious accommodation, which they found in Chislehurst. The house they chose had 21 rooms. By the time of the 1871 census, they employed a governess, nurse, cook, lady's maid, parlour maid, house maid, kitchen maid, nursery maid and coachman. It is surprising not to see a butler or housekeeper listed for such a sizeable household, but as the 1881 census shows a separate house for the coachman and his family, it's possible that this was missed out on the earlier count.

Elizabeth gave birth to ten children in total: Agnes in 1848, Emmeline in 1849, Edith in 1850, Theodore in 1852, Frederick in 1854, Ernest in 1856, Caroline in 1857. She seemed to get a bit of a break with the house move, the next child, Florence, not being born until late 1862, followed by Edgar, who was born on 6 August and died on 26 August 1864 – he was baptised and is buried in St Nicholas churchyard – and finally Lucy in 1867. Edith, Agnes, Florence and Caroline were all married from Lubbock Road, Edith to a local man, Edwin Arthur Jenner, in 1879. The weddings all took place at St Nicholas Church.

In 1886, FHJ sold a parcel of his land across the road and the name Camden Lodge went with it. The old house's new name became Oakbank, which is entirely appropriate given the number of acorns strewn around Lubbock Road every autumn.

Elizabeth died at their London home in 1889 but is buried alongside her infant son. Although now retired, FHJ annually took out his solicitor's license. He and his two unmarried daughters, Emmeline and Lucy, moved to Hove, in Sussex, downsizing to a house with merely 15 rooms.

Frederick Halsey Janson

I had a wonderful morning in the church office recently, looking at the archived parish magazine, ably assisted by the very helpful Peter Appleby. We eventually struck gold and found a reference to FHJ's role as churchwarden, a role he undertook for twenty-one years. These days, you are likely to undertake that task for about three years. Having searched the magazines around 1900, I eventually found what I was looking for in the 1886 volume – just when I was about to give up and Peter had had enough of going up and down his trusty stepladder.

'A Parochial Loss – We cannot help referring to the departure of a family from the neighbourhood, which was one of the oldest and truest friends of the Church and Parish of Chislehurst. Mr Janson has lived among us now upwards of twenty five years, and for twenty one years of that time he has exercised with unvarying courtesy and ability the office of Churchwarden. His genuine common sense as well as his legal acumen were often of great service to the Parish, and he was ever ready to place his talents at the disposal of the Parishioners. Few persons will be more missed than he. Generously hospitable to a wide circle of friends and acquaintances, most liberally charitable to all who stood in need of help, and to all good works, he set an example which had a very beneficial influence upon all with whom he came into contact. His departure with his family is a matter of real regret'.

I also found a reference to FHJ's 'excellent sacred recitations' for the Guild of St Nicholas, so it looks like he wasn't afraid of a little public speaking, either. FHJ played a prominent role in the defence of Chislehurst Commons against Lord Sydney, the Lord of the Manor. His confident public speaking may well have come in handy!

On 8 February 1913, FHJ received a congratulatory message from King George V, honouring him on reaching his 100th birthday. He died at Hove on 1 May that same year, leaving property in College Hill, London, as well as the Hove house, an estate valued in excess of £40,000.

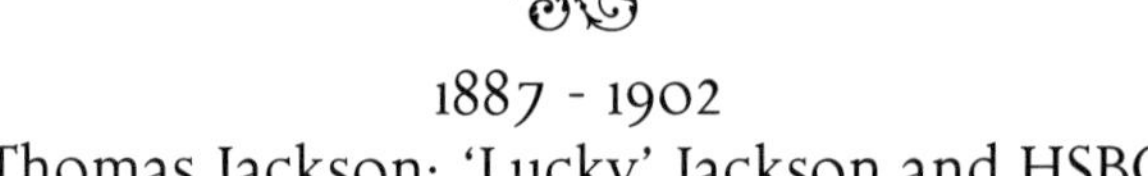

1887 - 1902
Thomas Jackson: 'Lucky' Jackson and HSBC

The residents of Oakbank looked undistinguished on a first pass through the census trail. Old Frederick Halsey Janson seemed a venerable City type and I wasn't expecting to find more of his ilk as time moved on. How wrong could I be? It is 1891, and there is a new occupant in the house, Thomas Jackson, soon to become Sir Thomas Jackson on account of his contribution to banking. Nathaniel Strode would surely have approved.

It appears that the Jackson family lived in Lubbock Road from at least 1887, dating their occupation from the birth of their seventh child and fifth daughter, Dorothy, in July of that year. Two sons followed, Walter Russell and Claude Stewart, born 1890 and 1892 respectively. When I noticed the older children had been born in Singapore and Hong Kong, and Thomas himself hailed from Ireland, my interest was aroused.

A Google search turned up the most fascinating stories and I quote here from *The Silver Bowl Biographies*, by Sharon Oddie Brown, and *The History of the Hong Kong and Shanghai Banking Corporation*, by Frank H. H. King.

Thomas Jackson was born in Carrigallen, Co. Leitrim. Jackson's father

Laying the foundation stone of Jackson's statue in Hong Kong, 1906

Unveiling of the statue, 24 February 1906

Sir Thomas 'Lucky' Jackson

Amelia Lydia Dare, Lady Jackson

The Jackson children, all born in Chislehurst, at their Hong Kong home, Creggan. Frm left to right, Dorothy, Walter, Claude.

is described as 'four generations from a landowner who around 1750 had lost all and was a teacher in the local school'. His mother was described as 'an educated woman of Huguenot ancestry'. Thomas began his career in banking with the Belfast branch of the Bank of Ireland. Four years later, he accepted a three-year position in the Far East as a clerk with the Agra and Masterman's Bank.

Thomas's first choice of employer in the Far East wasn't so propitious. The Agra and Masterman's Bank folded within three years of his arrival, but at least he had his foot in the door. His second job, with the Hong Kong and Shanghai Bank was unique. It was the first bank operating in the Far East to have been founded and headquartered in the territory that it served. Jackson's career with the Hong Kong and Shanghai Bank began on 6 August 1866.

Within a year, he had been promoted to accountant at Shanghai, a position that carried significant managerial responsibilities. By 1870, he was appointed to the post of manager of the Yokohama office. On 19 September 1871, Thomas married Amelia Lydia Dare, the daughter of a well known 'character' of Singapore, George Julias Dare. By 1876, Jackson was recognised as a hot young thing at the bank. He was made acting manager on the basis of his abilities and then, in 1877, was made chief manager. Not merely a born financier, he was known both for his charm and for his sincere concern for the people who worked for him. In a letter written by a colleague, Charles Addis, to his father, we have a glimpse of how he was regarded by his staff. 'What a fellow he is. Sound to the core. Straight in all his dealings, honest to the backbone, and with all a heart as tender as a woman's. Fiery, if you like, but I don't believe in a man who has not got a temper, it was a privilege to have received two years and more under such a chief. I believe I am a better man for knowing him.'

Jackson's timing was impeccable. He took over the bank just after it had endured several losses in the wake of a serious depression in both China and England. When he took over, the net profits were less than half a million dollars; when he retired, they stood at nearly three million. The bank was then able to finance the building of a new head office at what would become the most prime location in Hong Kong.

Part of what fuelled the rise of the bank's fortunes was Jackson's skill as a silver specialist and trader. One of Jackson's stated goals was to keep the bank on 'an even keel', which he did by keeping large silver deposits when almost no one else dared to, using them to make loans at a premium because there was no competition and thereby being able to accept all the contracts and advance loans which other companies couldn't handle because they didn't have adequate reserves to cover them. As a result of this skilful if risky management, he became known as 'Lucky Jackson'!

According to reminiscences by Thomas's daughter Amy, Jackson took up the post of manager of the London office in 1884, which would of course tie in with their residence in Chislehurst: a big house in an affluent neighbourhood within easy commuting distance of the City. T.J., as he was colloquially known, had a private office in Gracechurch Street. Amy tells us that he believed the secret of his success was that, whatever the situation, he could throw off all business once he got home, and could always sleep. Chislehurst must have had the desired effect! But twice after that date, when the Bank got into difficulties, he had to go back to Hong Kong to put things right.

It is at this point in the story where I feel sorry for my fellow woman. It is all very well counting Jackson as a resident of Lubbock Road, but in fact he was hardly here. Amy throws some light on what must have been a very difficult time for Amelia, or 'Minnie', as she was known in the family. 'Mother never came between father and his business or pried into anything. She undertook the immense hospitality he indulged in and she took complete control of her large family, choosing schools and paying all expenses. She had carte blanche on father's account and he trusted her completely'. 'If we needed money we must go to Mother who would help us if we deserved it.' It was clearly a strong and devoted marriage where each partner knew their role.

It can be relatively straightforward to gain a picture of men's lives. They joined clubs and societies. Announcements about their patronages were made in The Gazette. In the nineteenth century, fulsome sketches were written about 'Leading Men of London', and obituaries include details of schools and parentage. About women, a picture is less easy to glean. Imagine, then, my delight, upon returning to Sharon Oddie Brown's Silver Bowl website and learning that a batch of letters had been discovered in an Irish bog in the 1960s and transcribed on the internet!

These were letters from Mrs Jackson senior, T.J.'s mother Eliza, to her son, describing events back home. Several commented on his wife and family. She writes in August 1887, 'I must congratulate you on the birth of your daughter [Dorothy, at Chislehurst].....By last account, Mother and Child were doing well. I never feared for your family; you went East on a purely unselfish errand; and I knew that God (and several servants) would watch over the dear ones that you left behind. You have had a roving time since you left England. May God bring you safely back. You did not mention if you have succeeded in putting things to rights.....You were always the luck of the Bank since you joined it.'

In September 1887 comes something of a letter of martyrdom! 'Poor Minnie is greatly disappointed at your prolonged absence. She wrote asking my advice what she should do. I advised her just to stay quietly where she is.... she will not feel lonely when she has her children about her. I think you did right to stay in the East, when you found that your services were required......but on no account prolong your stay beyond the time appointed; you cannot stay all your life in the East, nor sacrifice yourself altogether. Although we approve of what you have done, we feel the disappointment very much. Every delay makes the chance less to me of seeing you again in this life, but duty should always come before pleasure.' How very Victorian!

The sense of separation is highlighted again in 1893. Eliza writes to her daughter in law, 'Dear Minnie,......On the one hand it is hard for you and Tom to be separated for so long a period; on the other it is just as hard for you to divide your family and leave three of them behind. [The youngest three would only have been 6, 3 and 1] Think what you would feel if death claimed any of them in your absence; think also of the pity it would be, to break up your beautiful home on which you have spent so much.......I am sorry to learn that the children are still suffering from whooping cough.'

Eliza obviously has an axe to grind on this issue and writes also to her son, 'I fear that Minnie will perhaps come out to the East, but do not you consent to that. How could she steer off and leave her family behind and the expense of leaving them out [in Hong Kong] would be ruinous; besides interrupting the schooling of the younger ones. I have every confidence that you will succeed with your present mission.....' I bet she does; I'm not sure in Minnie's shoes I would like such a controlling mother-in-law! However, judging by the charming family photograph taken of the Chislehurst-born children in the garden of the family home 'Creggan', on the Hong Kong Peak, it looks like Minnie got her way!

Eliza's concern for her family did not fade with time; in 1893, she writes to her son, 'There is one thing [Hardly!] that I must write you about – your two grown up daughters are going out to see you; no doubt they will meet with admirers and offers of marriage. I charge you never give them to wicked or ungodly men; no matter how great the temporal advantages seem to be. Neither wealth nor rank, nor beauty can make amends for the want of the blessing of God; and that blessing the wicked cannot have.' We get some insight as to how the family spent their lives away from their parents overseas; Grandparents obviously came in useful, so some things never change. 'Beatrice, Tom, Julius are to spend their Easter vacation here, the Christmas vacation they are to spend with friends in England. Minnie did not like them to cross the Channel at that time of year.'

Back in London, Jackson was made chairman of the London Committee, with a salary of £1,500 per annum. He was knighted on 8 July 8 1899. Three years, later, on 4 August 1902, Sir Thomas Jackson received the additional honour of a baronetcy, and chose to retire at Stansted House in Essex, an estate of one hundred acres.

On 24 February 1906, a bronze statue of Jackson facing the Bank was unveiled in Statue Square, Hong Kong, which is adjacent to Jackson Road. The family attended the unveiling. I was very grateful to my roving reporter Jo Reddy for the current photographs sent direct from Hong Kong, but am thrilled to have come across contemporary photographs of the event.

Working to the last, or perhaps at a pre-Christmas gathering, 'Lucky Jackson' died at his desk at 9 Gracechurch Street, reading the morning mail on 21 December 1915, leaving a fortune worth over £128,000.

But not all the Lubbock Road sons were 'lucky'. Claude, Thomas's youngest child, fell victim to the First World War at Ypres in Belgium, as a Captain in the Coldstream Guard in 1917. Claude had trained at Sandhurst as an officer from the age of 19, and had only been married for one year when he died. He is buried at Tyne Cot Cemetery.

1902- 1942
Samuel Worksett: Glovemaker to the Masses

The final resident of Oakbank that I can trace, taking us right up to the Second World War, was London glovemaker Samuel Worksett. Arthur Battle, the village baker, wrote in *Edwardian Chislehurst* that: 'Worksett of The London Glove Company was in residence during his time of delivering bread to the big houses in Lubbock Road'. Samuel Worksett was not a man of any particular distinction, but his fortune was entirely self-made.

Samuel was the son of an agricultural labourer from Woodham Ferrers in Essex. Samuel may have had a tough upbringing; he was born in 1849, and his father and family breadwinner died when Samuel was only four years old.

By 1881, things had moved on for Samuel: in 1879 he had married Louise Mengedoht, the daughter of a Hanoverian steward, and was living in Fairlop Road, Leyton. Impressively, he is listed as a Glover Master at the age of only 32, employing two men and three boys. He and Louise had a baby daughter called Daisy and a general servant. Intriguingly, their house is called Daisy Villa; did they call their daughter after the house or the house after the baby?

Over the next ten years, six more children were born, two little boys after five daughters. They had moved to Rulford Road, Streatham, and Samuel is now listed as a wholesale and retail Glover. The children have a governess and Louise is running a household that consists of a cook and three housemaids. Their neighbours are engineers and solicitors, typical of the growing wealthy middle class of this era.

Business must have been doing well, as the family stayed in the area and moved to Mount Ephraim Road, number 24. Samuel is now a Glover and Hosiery Merchant. A further three children have been born.

The need for space would have been paramount with a growing family. The 1911 census sees them at Oakbank and also reveals sadness. One of their children, Frank, died in 1907 here in Chislehurst. However, Herbert, aged 8, and Laurence, aged 7 in 1911, were born at Oakbank.

The London Glove Company was thriving and Samuel was made an alderman of the City of London, representing the Worshipful Company of Glovers. His advertisements for beautiful gloves for both men and women are plentiful in London illustrated magazines. Interestingly, court cases are also plentiful, with young women being prosecuted for stealing gloves from Samuel's outlets.

Young Stanley Worksett, age 23, the first son after his five older sisters, worked for his father as a drapery warehouse clerk; Samuel obviously believed in learning the business from the bottom up. The daughters are all at home and the family employ a cook, a nurse, a parlour maid, two house maids and a kitchen maid. In Oakbank Cottage next door, there is Samuel's gardener, his family and a nineteen-year-old boarder from Croydon who is also employed in the grounds of the big house.

Stanley fought in the war, joining the 7th Battalion Royal Fusiliers in 1915. After a period in the Officers' Training Corps he became a 2nd Lieutenant in the Special Reserve of Officers. Ernest, born in 1896 also joined up in 1915 and became an officer. I can't imagine what emotions

must have gone through Samuel and Louise's minds as their sons marched away to war. Not just their sons, but the livelihood of the family business, was at stake.

Thankfully, their stories are those of survival: Ernest was awarded a Victory Medal from the Gallipoli campaign. It's certainly good to see that not all the boys of Lubbock Road were slaughtered in the theatre of war. From his eldest sister's probate information, I can tell that Ernest lived to be a retired glove merchant, the family business still trading ahead of significant changes in fashions and a decline in wearing such a variety of gloves. Stanley, too, was granted probate of his sister's assets after her death in Sevenoaks Hospital; he is listed as a Commission Man in the Stock Exchange, so perhaps he didn't warm to the hosiery business as much as his younger brother.

Oakbank must have witnessed at least four grand weddings. Beatrice married in 1909. Constance married in 1912; she married Ronald Vinson from Raggleswood, the house next door! The Vinson fruit-farming business is still thriving today. The family originally farmed at Halfway Street in Sidcup, and there is a road near there named after the family, Vinson Close. Both Muriel and Phyllis married in 1928. I hope they all wore the most splendid gloves! Louise appears to have married in later life, and Daisy and Ethel remained single.

Samuel died at Oakbank in 1933, aged 84, leaving £7,685, and Louise died on holiday in Llandudno with Daisy in 1942. Daisy died aged 78, and Ethel was 93 when she passed away.

There is no evidence of war service for Herbert, but he is listed as an executor of Stanley's will, working as a builder.

Herbert and Laurence, the youngest sons, were were too young for First World War, but Laurence, the youngest and the last child to be born at Oakbank, fought and survived Second World War. He was a Colonel in the Royal Army Ordnance Corps, responsible for the demolition of enemy positions. Awarded an OBE in 1945 for his services in North West Europe, he also gained a Royal Aero Club Aviators' Certificate. Somehow, the Worksett world was showing signs of coming full circle: Laurence was listed as a farmer when he signed up for active service.

In the aerial photograph taken in 1937, Oakbank itself was still standing, but the family had grown and moved on. When Louise Worksett, already a widow, died during the war, this was the end of an era, the beginning of the end of the original grand houses of Lubbock Road. Developers moved in, and the site is now occupied by more contemporary detached homes. The name Oakbank still survives, as Oakbank Cottage, tucked away on the bend of the road.

Camden Hill (now Great Ash)

5. Camden Hill

1864 - 1880
Henry Clutton: Imperial Architect

Camden Hill, or Great Ash as it is now known, was another glorious journey of discovery. It's the story of an architect who should have had more distinction and would have made a fortune had his designs been executed. Sadly, religious prejudice thwarted his ambition. In telling the tale of Henry Clutton, I am pleased to find he nevertheless left an indelible mark on Chislehurst.

Clutton was born in 1819 in Surrey. On the death of his father, when he was only fifteen, Henry was articled to the architect Edward Blore, in whose office he remained for a decade. Between 1845 and 1856, Henry's career advanced with commissions for country houses, Anglican churches, schools and colleges. He became prominent in architectural circles as a founder member of the Architectural Museum, a member of the Ecclesiological Society and a fellow of the RIBA. His major publication, Remarks with illustrations on the Domestic Architecture of France, from the accession of Charles VI to the demise of Louis XII, established Clutton as something of an authority on fifteenth-century French buildings. In 1853, his collaboration with William Burges culminated in their winning a competition to design Lille Cathedral in the thirteenth-century French Gothic style. The first stone was laid in 1854, but Blore and Clutton argued, and their partnership came to a sharp conclusion in 1856. The plans for Lille were aborted. Clutton's daughter Margaret sees it slightly differently, and reflects on the sacrifices her father made in the name of religion: Clutton had felt it only honourable to tell the Bishop in Lille that he was Anglican, and for this reason the plans were returned to him.

The year 1856 marked a major turning point in Clutton's career. He converted to Roman Catholicism and was listed by W. Gordon Gorman as a 'notable' convert to the faith. Thereafter, commissions from the Anglican establishment ceased. Clutton was entrusted with the restoration of Salisbury Cathedral, but the completion of the Chapter House coincided with his reception into the Catholic church. Before beginning the work, he told the Bishop he was no longer a member of the Church of England, and such was the prejudice against Catholics in those days, the work was instantly withdrawn. His timing was less than perfect! Clutton relied instead on the patronage of country house clients, the Dukes of Bedford and the Roman Catholic hierarchy. He took on commissions for poor Catholic congregations such as St Francis of Assisi, Pottery Lane, London, and an Italian Renaissance cloister of the Oratorians at Edgbaston, Birmingham. His country house work can be seen in varied style at Hatherop House, Gloucestershire, Minley Manor, Hampshire, Wrotham Park in Hertfordshire, and the Water Tower at Clivedon above the Thames.

Clutton made a significant Roman Catholic alliance in his marriage in 1860 to Caroline Alice Ryder, daughter of George Ryder, another convert. Alice, as she was known, was 21 years his junior. Cardinal Henry Manning was her uncle. If the name Manning is familiar to Chislehurst residents, you may be thinking of the Manning and Anderdon almshouses built in 1881, endowed by other nieces of Cardinal Manning. Henry and Alice started married life in Golden Square, Westminster, and their first three children were born there.

At this point in the story, I am indebted to the wonderful find by my research ally Yvonne Auld, of a typewritten book, *Memories of my Childhood*, by Margaret M. Clutton, Henry's seventh child (there were to be nine in total). I devoured the text in the Historic Collections in Bromley, and the photocopier worked overtime on that day, I recall! The book, once you get past the many reverential references and descriptions of all things holy, reveal in glorious detail life inside Camden Hill, the house that Clutton designed and had built for his family in Chislehurst, up a private drive from the dirt track which later became Lubbock Road.

The book was, heaven forgive me, a real temptation to me. I had to get inside the house itself. It still stands proud on the hillside, hidden from view and now split into several flats. I couldn't just go and knock on doors... or at least I didn't feel I could. The next piece of the jigsaw fell into place over one of my many fruitful cups of coffee with my ever-patient next-door neighbour. Poor Viv, she has had to listen to many moments of my historical – or almost hysterical [sic] – excitement over the years, but this time my excitement resonated with her, too. It turned out that Viv's young son had a school friend who lived in one of the flats. The school-gate network is a powerful thing and, one quick email later, copied to another resident, I found myself arranging a further cuppa inside the oldest part of the original house.

I got a full tour of the flat and took in its stunning views. There is still a remarkable feeling of serenity, high above the bustle of the road below.

However, even more exciting, my new friend Jill produced an article from Country Life magazine dated 1979, and some photocopies of a thesis written by Ms P. Hunting on the life of Henry Clutton. Together, these articles completed the very significant story of Henry Clutton and his contribution to Chislehurst. It features, of course, Nathaniel Strode, but also the Empress Eugénie in her mourning garb.

In April 1864, Clutton was approached by Strode, who admired Clutton's style of building – this tallies with Nathaniel's love of all things French – and wanted to introduce it among the persons who bought sites on the developing estate. Clutton himself was given the choice of two sites on which to build for himself a red-brick house, designed to be the prototype of the future development of Camden Park. But Strode's plan went awry; some of his neighbours (Winch? Lubbock?) were displeased by the sale of such a prominent site to Clutton, and were unenthusiastic about the emerging house. Strode requested that Clutton pull down his house and rebuild it at the foot of the hill. Clutton agreed, if Strode would finance the rebuilding. In Strode's absence abroad, Clutton's house was completed in the original position at the top of the hill. Strode registered his objection by erecting a palisade outside Clutton's garden, to shut out his view from Camden Place. According to *Country Life*, Clutton was indebted to the former Emperor Napoleon III for intervening in the wrangle between himself and Strode, but this seems unlikely to me, given the timing of the exiled emperor's arrival at Chislehurst as late as 1871, whereas Clutton was building Camden Hill in 1864!

The development of the Camden Place Estate continued uninfluenced by Clutton. Camden Hill's overall position is probably why, in future conveyances, Strode ensured there was a clause 'not to erect any building which could be visible from the first-floor windows of Camden Place without consent in writing from Strode himself'. If you see the house from the 'new' road, at Raggleswood, Camden Hill dominates the skyline, but from Lubbock Road, you wouldn't know it was there.

Margaret Clutton, also known as Daisy (by her brothers, teasingly referring to the name of the family's cow that grazed in the meadow on the edge of the park), describes Camden Hill and her life in Chislehurst in beautiful detail. 'People took long drives in an open carriage just for the pleasure of the fresh air and scenery and also to make sure the coachman had enough to do!' Below her bedroom window was a wide sweep at the top of the carriage drive, ending in front of the pillared double porch; and

Henry Clutton

beyond the bushes were the iron gate leading into Camden Park, with its grassy slopes and tall trees.

All the rooms faced south or west. Margaret says herself that it was not a beautiful country house nor a magnificent mansion but a house where children could lead a free and happy life. They could 'run and shout in the corridors without rebuke, be untidy and dishevelled, even muddy as long as we appeared well groomed and gentle and well mannered when we passed the enclosure doors'. She describes playing games based on Robinson Crusoe and Swiss Family Robinson, playing at highwaymen, based on Dick Turpin, but best of all dressing up and pretending to say Mass, usually ending with a furious fight between penitent and confessor!

Mass was said in the house. A room near the hall was reserved as a chapel, on the ground floor, with a window high in the wall making the room dark and catacomb-like. Jill and I think this is now a bathroom! Alice had four brothers, three of whom were priests, Margaret clearly recalls them all playing cricket on the lawn! She also remembers the visits of her great uncle, Cardinal Manning dressed in rich red robes and they all had strawberries for tea; I guess it didn't matter if the juice stained his garb! She watched the summer manoeuvres of volunteers in Camden Park; the drilling, drumming and trumpetery were vivid memories; Her brother joined them as an officer.

Her eldest brother became a lieutenant in the Royal Artillery after serving a cadetship at Woolwich; he went to Gibraltar but died in 1909. Another brother became a naval cadet at Dartmouth and brought rats home as pets!

Her mother taught the girls to read, write and sew, but they had a governess in the schoolroom. The eldest girls went next door to Miss Amos's school at Coed-bel for music, drawing and German.

I hate to dispute the work of Tom Bushell, our late eminent local historian, but I have three sources that say the mortuary chapel at St Mary's, Chislehurst, was designed by Clutton and not the French architect Destailleur, as quoted by Bushell. (Destailleur designed the final resting place of the Emperor Napoleon III at St Michael's Abbey in Farnborough, Hampshire). According to Penelope Hunting, Empress Eugénie engaged Clutton within three months of Napoleon's death. The Empress was fond of the Clutton children and, like Clutton himself, she was a devout Catholic. When in London, she worshipped at the Jesuit church in Farm Street, to which Clutton had added the Sacred Heart Chapel in 1858. Her familiarity with Clutton personally, and his work, was adequate reason for commissioning him to design the memorial chapel at Chislehurst. In the little booklet *The Wood on the Stony Hill*, by Rev T.P. O'Beirne, Clutton is mentioned as the architect of the chapel, and Margaret refers to her father undertaking this commission in her Childhood Memories. It was one of Clutton's few commissions from the Catholic laity, and he refused to accept payment for his work, giving the money instead to the Diocese of Southwark.

Margaret Clutton has distinct memories of the widowed Empress. The Clutton children occasionally met her on the Common or outside church; she greeted them kindly, bending down to kiss them. However another memory is even more distinctive. One morning, their nurse insisted – unusually – that they stand along the road leading from the station to the Camden Park gates. There was no crowd, just a handful of people, waiting. Then, under the water tower arch on the crest of the road, there appeared a carriage with outriders. There was Queen Victoria, a solitary figure in black seated in an open carriage. The Queen disappeared through the gates, under what Margaret describes as 'the heavy foliage of that sinister looking avenue'!

By the end of 1879, Margaret describes her father as completely blind, although his other senses became more acute. He could sense which child was in the room by their individual step. His sense of touch was marvellous: he had beautiful hands with tapering fingers. He walked about the house without a stick and without hesitation, though he did not trust himself outside alone. He had a pageboy, 'Buttons', who saw to his needs at table. Buttons sat patiently for long hours, silent though ready to answer questions. Henry was read to every day, *The Times*, *The Pall Mall*, *St James's Gazette*, *The Spectator*, *The Illustrated London News* and *The Graphic*, as well as *Punch*.

There was great sorrow when Camden Hill was sold in 1880, but it was better for Henry to live in London near friends, where he could attend functions and go to church to hear sermons.

Henry Clutton died in June 1893 at his brother's house at Brookside, West Drayton, Middlesex, and is buried in the family tomb at Mortlake.

Camden Hill passed into the hands of a wealthy family of shipbuilders from Hull, the Gibsons. The family is listed in the 1911 census and the house has 24 rooms. Tragedy struck when a son, Philip, was killed in France in 1916. The family grave at St Nicholas is white marble and clearly identifies the house they lived in. A daughter gained some distinction locally: her father left her all the contents of his library in his will. That aroused my interest (and particularly as she was called Dorothea, one of my Christian names). Dorothea Gibson was a scholar and you will find her work in Webb's *History*, under the heading of the origin and meaning of places, fields and woods in and around Chislehurst.

6. Coed-bel

1865-1992
A Welshman, Schoolgirls, Prisoners and Apprentices

A mysterious name to a somewhat mysterious house. A house that had a remarkable place in the history of the road, holding its own secrets within its walls before it was demolished, and certainly a spooky place in the memories of any adult who was a child in the road during the Seventies.

I had two unexpected treats in store with this piece of research, and two very special people to be grateful to, for opening up the doors to Coed-bel. First – as she was bound to appear on these pages at some point – is my own mother. To those who don't know her, my mother is the world's best befriender. Luckily for me, she is as enthusiastic about my love for Lubbock Road as I am, so when she got chatting to strangers in church one Sunday, albeit in faraway Northumberland, it came as no surprise that I received a phone call with the telephone number of a lady who used to live at Coed-bel. It transpired that 'Gill' had been the daughter of the YMCA warden who ran the hostel for War Office apprentices at Coed-bel from 1947, and she now lived in Canterbury. A swift phone call – I think her husband thought I was a little mad – and then lunch at their house was arranged. That was an upgrade on coffee!

The second debt that I owe is to Mr David Miller. Dave, as he allows me to call him, now that we have got past formal introductions, is a gentleman in his eighties who used to live in Mottingham, and sheltered in the Caves during the war. Dave has an active memory and recalls his childhood mishaps climbing walls, scrumping for apples in the gardens of the 'big houses' and fishing for salamander in the pond at Beechcroft (now Livingstone House). Dave has a passion for antiques and collectibles and has made it his business to collect legal documents relating to Chislehurst when they have come up for sale on eBay. Dave bought three indentures relating to the original purchase of Coed-bel. In my research for the origins of the name of Coed-bel, I found Dave on the same thread of messages to a BBC Wales local history page! Dave and I have exchanged many e-mails over the last few years, I have been treated to lunch at his home and he has been here to one of those 'big houses' for afternoon tea. I would never have made headway without Dave and his indentures.

I knew from *Kelly's Street Directories* that William Mostyn was living at

Coed-bel in 1865. He appears on the 1871 census as an inspector of the Exchequer, married to Clementia. There were no children. Maps of the road show Coed-bel to be a particularly large site. Dave's indentures were dated 1865, and showed a further purchase in 1866. The land was purchased from Nathaniel Strode. The most exciting image for me was the map contained within the conveyance. It was hand-drawn and very boldly named the road Lubbock Road. This was first time I had seen mention of the name of the road as early as this.

William Mostyn of 15 Thurloe Square bought the first two acre plot of land for £1,000. He bought a further small strip of land to the west for £50 six months later and, finally, with his wife and her uncle/ guardian, Captain Arthur William Jerningham R.N., they purchased a further two acres for another £500 each. Coed-bel was built on these combined plots.

William was born in Worcestershire, the seventh son of Sir Edward Mostyn, Baron Talacre of Flint. (No wonder our William became a civil servant! With six brothers to distribute any wealth between, he would need his own income!) There is a Coed-bel on Mostyn Road, Talacre; the name means wood or forest, and is a 'green' graveyard.

The Mostyns were a Catholic family, as was Clementia's. I found Clementia's sister married in January 1896, the daughter of the late Edmund Jerningham, at St Mary's Roman Catholic Church, Chislehurst. Their uncle was Admiral Jerningham. In 1835, he served on HMS Excellent and HMS Wellesley, in the First Opium War. He was attached to Queen Victoria's personal guard during the Chartist disturbances. A man of some personal wealth and with a taste for adventure and travel! Gill was to tell me later that the grounds of Coed-bel had some spectacular specimen trees, including a rare tulip tree, one of only six in the country at the time, which a Kew Gardens inspector had once investigated. Could it be that the Admiral had brought a sapling or seeds back from his Mediterranean and Far East travels? Kew Gardens, sadly, had no record of any such visit to Chislehurst and the current house owners cannot identify any trees out of the ordinary, bar the substantial redwoods and Cedar of Lebanon at the front elevation near the road.

William and Clementia may have had dreams of producing a family similar to those in which they had grown up, but there seems to be no evidence of that. They moved from Chislehurst to Surrey without family. Perhaps they spent their time gardening! William died in 1909, leaving £13,403 to his wife, who died in 1925; that was some fortune!

Coed-bel house

View from the house

Coed-bel from the road

Coed-bel lawn

Willow Lodge and Coed-bel from the lower end of Lubbock Road

School Library, 1877-1941

Coed-bel School lacrosse team

Royal Ordnance Apprentices, 1960s

Like other 'big houses' in the road, Coed-bel continued its life as an institution and took on various guises over the next 100 years. The house became a school for girls in 1877, when Miss Katherine Amos moved her school from Leicester. She remained Headmistress until 1910, when her niece Miss Winifred Hamilton Fox – who had been a pupil at the school since she was ten – took over. Miss Beatrix Fox Batten – a renowned local character, Girton graduate and Red Cross Commandant during the First World War – taught maths at the school. In 1941, the school was evacuated to Somerset and never returned to Chislehurst. Originally, it was almost entirely a boarding school, with very few day pupils, but after the War, more day boarders were taken until in the 1930s there were more day pupils than boarders. The top lawns were tennis courts, which I imagine had already been laid out by the Mostyns; there was also a court at the slightly lower level, and another at the bottom of the lawns outside the drawing room. The greenhouse (Mostyn's passion?) was the school laboratory; and the bungalow by the garages – the former coach house, now Willow Lodge – was the sanatorium. There was no adequate heating and in the winter the girls nearly froze; they wore gloves and overcoats to keep warm! This was to become a recurring theme in many recollections from Coed-bel residents. It must have been a draughty old place!

The darkest period of Coed-bel's story is the Second World War, when it became a prisoner of war camp. It has proved almost impossible to gain any information about this period, as the English Heritage archives reveal very little. It appears it was a work camp for the duration of the war, holding mostly Italian prisoners. There is mention in an article in *Cockpit* of foreign prisoners being noticed as they went to pick artichokes in the fields at Red Hill. It must have been requisitioned by the government and became the responsibility of the War Office.

After the war, in 1947, Coed-bel opened to provide accommodation for the apprentices and trainees who lived too far away to travel daily to defence sites at Woolwich, Fort Halsted or Aquila. When the Royal Ordnance Factory Apprentice Scheme was extended, it was necessary to find a hostel to accommodate the annual intake of thirty boys. Coed-bel was chosen, but it was in poor condition after its days as a prison camp, with dry rot in many places, old boilers providing for too few radiators, and practically no heating in the bedrooms (Now I feel really sorry for the boarders at the school). Crises with peeling paint and overcrowding were slowly overcome, with newly acquired accommodation in Lower Camden and tins of paint.

The hostel was managed by the YMCA and was home to an ever-changing number of boys from various parts of the country. With different backgrounds, ambitions, outlooks and talents, all worked, studied, argued and played together, in what was described as an exhilarating, lively and friendly place. Gill was the daughter of the YMCA warden on site. 'Played' seemed to be an operative word, as Gill told me of the escapades that the boys got up to: chiefly, 'borrowing' signs to use as temporary mascots! One such target was a teapot sign from a café at Biggin Hill. Another caused a bit more of a stir; this was the 'Grasshopper Case', when Martins Bank, at the top of Summer Hill, took a week or so to notice that they had lost their metal grasshopper emblem. Things looked rather bad when a barrister was engaged to prosecute the culprits! Surprisingly, the usually stern apprentice's supervisor claimed that all six were 'angels, really' and were only doing the same as students elsewhere had done, to gain a mascot. They got off with a nominal fine of 2s 6d each.

At a party held at Coed-bel in 1962, the assistant director of engineering services realised there were problems that could not be overcome by mere tins of paint. There was a need for modernisation and change. Outline planning permission had been received for a new purpose-built hostel, and plans were in place to leave Coed-bel in the next three years. The apprentices and Gill's family left the site in 1965, after which time it remained empty. The site was condemned in 1972, but lay rotting for many more years before it was finally demolished, and new homes were built by Bovis in 1992. Several people have told me with glee of their forays into the grounds through the barbed wire, to play various daring games and, in gentler moments, to pick blackberries. William and Clementia would have smiled.

The sanatorium also played a significant role in providing beds for wounded Belgian soldiers in 1914, and it became a cottage home of rest for women and girls under the auspices of the Elizabeth Garrett Anderson Hospital up until 1932. When I was shown around what is now Willow Lodge, I was also shown the medicine bottles that were unearthed during basement excavations.

Gill's insights into the road are worth noting. She recalls the Catholic nunnery over the road. She also commented that Lubbock Road was known as Millionaire's Row, with a distinct split between the grand and the less grand at the church!

Willow Lodge, the former lodge of Coed-bel and Red Cross Hospital 1914-18

Two views of Granite Lodge

7. Granite Lodge

1869 - 1934
The Freese Family and General Gordon

Granite Lodge was first occupied by Frederick and Octavia Freese, who lived for over sixty-six years in Lubbock Road. This is a story that has kept unravelling, revealing distinctive connections and a wonderful twist in the final turn. Granite Lodge is entirely different in structure to any other house in the road; I have not been able to find the name of the architect although the house is locally listed. The entire façade is made of hexagonal medallions of granite and flint, which is most unusual.

Frederick Freese and his wife Octavia moved to Chislehurst from Milton, in Gravesend, in 1869. Frederick William was born in 1838 in Broad Street, London. His father Philip was an insurance broker born in Middlesex, who raised his family in Hackney; his wife died three years after Frederick was born. Frederick became an exchange broker and also had a home in London at Great Winchester Street. The plot for Granite Lodge was purchased from Nathaniel Strode for £1,195, with strict instructions that the house should be built the same as other houses on the adjoining land. Perhaps that just meant a detached dwelling, because Granite Lodge is certainly unlike any other house nearby!

The couple's move to Chislehurst is curious because they were so closely associated with their Gravesend community: committed Evangelical Christians, they ran the ragged school there. Was it the railway and its regular service to the City that brought them here (Gravesend didn't have a train link to London until 1886)? I am totally indebted to the research endeavours of Yvonne Auld for this story. She was researching the history of Merton Court School in Sidcup and, quite by chance, came across the obituary of Octavia Freese in the local paper. I was travelling home on the train from the theatre in town when Yvonne sent me the message; however, I only had my BlackBerry with me, and couldn't open the attachments! I could only read, frustrated, Yvonne's telling me that she had found a lengthy article about Octavia's one hundredth birthday, which included a photograph of the lady herself. I didn't think I could get through the door and onto my computer fast enough, but finally here I was, and there it was, a particularly full account of Octavia's life, and her reflections on Chislehurst, Lubbock Road in particular.

Octavia, as you can surmise from her name, was the eighth child of fourteen! She was born in Homerton, Middlesex. Her father, James Edmeston, was an architect and prolific writer of some 2,000 hymns, the best-known being 'Lead Us, Heavenly Father, Lead Us'. This appeared in Hymns Ancient and Modern, compiled by Canon Murray, Rector of St Nicholas, Chislehurst, was this the connection which drew the Freese family to Chislehurst? I would love to think that Edmeston designed Granite Lodge, but he died in 1867, two years prior to the move.

Within the detail of the article was the fascinating piece of information that Octavia was a confidante of General Gordon, of Chinese and Khartoum fame. Well, here was a name of real distinction! In Gravesend, they had been near neighbours when General Gordon lived at Fort House.

The Freeses were deeply committed to charitable works. They were the epitome of the well-off middle class working with the poverty-stricken. Many people at that time lived on the streets, including thousands of children. The journalist Henry Mayhew's *London Labour and the London Poor*, published in 1865, catalogued in great detail the condition of the London poor, and it had a profound impact on Evangelical Christians.

The Freeses were one such Evangelical couple; James Edmeston had served as a church warden at St Barnabas in Homerton and was a strong supporter and frequent visitor to the London Orphan Asylum. His influence on his daughter was indelible. Octavia and Frederick met General Gordon in 1866 and were immediately impressed by his earnestness. Frederick urged Gordon to become involved in the Evangelical social work of Gravesend. They ran a soup kitchen, visited the sick, and established the local ragged school. Gordon taught the most needy children, provided clothing and food, and organised pensions for the elderly. He opened up Fort House to the poor, and opened large tracts of army land for use as allotments. The influence of the Freeses was significant; they spent many hours talking with him about the practical outworking of the Gospel. It was Frederick who introduced Gordon to the ragged school.

Gordon was very fond of children and especially devoted to Octavia's two sons, Frederick and Francis, born in 1863 and 1865 respectively. Gordon was an occasional visitor to Granite Lodge and he used to bury half crowns in the garden for the boys to dig up, but he would not let them dig until the following morning. One of Gordon's visits to Chislehurst was at the time of the funeral of former Emperor Napoleon III in January 1873. He also went to church at Chislehurst one Sunday and gave his opinion of the sermon! If only we could identify the minister at fault, for I suspect Gordon's comments were less than complimentary. The family used to attend St George's at Bickley before Christ Church was built. Mrs Freese used to send the children out before the sermon; was it such fire and damnation, or just not very child-friendly? It was on their way home that Mrs Freese tells of meeting Empress Eugénie who took a fancy to one of Mrs Freese's daughters. The Empress admired her pretty curls and kissed her. Far from being complimented, the daughter considered it a great affront (how very British)! Another daughter, Ethel, was a god-daughter of General Gordon, and her name, with those of his other god-children, is written inside his bible, now housed at Windsor Castle.

Not surprisingly, given her father's talent for hymn writing, Octavia was an active member of the Christ Church choir and her husband, too, joined in. How very convenient, as Granite Lodge is directly across the road from the church. I can't find any reference to the Freeses continuing good works in Chislehurst, but I can't believe they gave it all up.

Gordon left for the Sudan in January 1874 and sent a post card to Octavia; it reads: "23.1.74 Isaiah 35 Goodbye Gordon". The biblical reference is: 'The wilderness and the solitary place shall be glad for them; and the desert shall rejoice and blossom as the rose'. It is not clear if the friendship continued into the next decade, but as we know General Gordon did not have reason to rejoice in Khartoum; he was besieged and killed at the end of January 1885.

By the 1881 census, the Freeses had a young family, Frederick was in his early forties and was working in the City. Octavia was six years his junior. Their last two children, daughters Ada and Mabel, were born at Granite Lodge. Maybe pregnancy altered Octavia's persona a little, but I was intrigued to find references to her at this time under the heading of telepathic hallucinations! In September 1881, she had a curious dream, so vivid that she seemed to see it, she writes. 'My two boys of 18 and 16 were staying in the Black Forest, under the care of Dr Fresenius. My husband and I were staying at St Leonards, and on Saturday night I woke at about 12 o'clock, rather before as I heard it strike, having just seen vividly a dark night on a mountain, and my eldest boy lying on his back at the bottom of some steep place, his eyes wide open and saying, "Good-bye, mother and father, I shall never see you again." I woke with a feeling of anxiety, and the next morning when I told it to my husband, though we both agreed it was absurd to be anxious, yet we would write and tell the boys we hoped they

Granite Lodge

would never go out alone after dark. To my surprise my eldest boy, to whom I wrote the dream, wrote back expressing his great astonishment, for on that Saturday night he was coming home over the mountains, past 11 o'clock; it was pitch black, and he slipped and fell down some 12 feet or so, and landed on his back, looking up to the sky. However, he was not much hurt and soon picked himself up and got home all right. He did not say what thoughts passed through his mind as he fell!

Frederick Snr died on 5 August 1898, aged 60. It wasn't stress that got him but chronic nephritis, the curse of the water works; he died at home with Octavia by his side.

In December 1899, Ada married Ernest Slade, the son of local benefactor Adolphus Slade (Slade owned much of the land on what is now Belmont, and gave money towards the building of the Annunciation Church). Ernest was an Exchange broker, like Ada's father. They went to live in St Leonards. There were no children from this union; in 1912, Ada passed away, aged 46, in a diabetic coma, an illness from which she had suffered for five years.

The second son, Francis Shirley Freese, didn't seem to have quite the same work ethic as his parents or older brother. I did find him listed as a merchant returning from New York in 1891, but the 1911 census lists his occupation as 'nothing at present'. In June 1912, I found him on the

Octavia Freese, aged 100

SS Zealander from Sydney, Australia, bound for Hawaii, then home via Jamaica. He is listed as having no occupation and with Granite Lodge still as his home address. He has no war record and in fact I found him travelling again in 1915, this time as a student inbound from the West Indies. Maybe he settled down to work on his return; his death certificate lists him as a retired bill broker. I think there is a deeper story that I just haven't found here; he passed away in July 1921, aged just 56, lacking his mother's genes for longevity. Francis died of an aortic aneurism and a respiratory obstruction. His death certificate also concludes that he was suffering from 'exhaustion'. He died in the Cray Valley Hospital with his sister Ethel at his side. He left an estate worth just over £16,000.

Octavia reached her 100th birthday in March 1934. Wearing purple velvet and cream lace, she courteously answered the questions of a Kentish Times reporter. She was looking forward to a quiet family party; she was described then as frail but keen. Octavia died less than six months after that 100th birthday. She had sustained a broken leg while on holiday not long before and had been almost incapable since. She was buried in St Nicholas churchyard alongside her husband.

Ethel died in 1937 at Granite Lodge, leaving her estate – worth £4,500 – to her younger sister Mabel. It's interesting that she used Cecil Antony

Nussey as her solicitor. The Nussey family of lawyers have a long-standing and worthy connection with Chislehurst. John Nussey some years earlier had saved the Commons from enclosure (and hence saved Chislehurst for what we have today). As Octavia herself said on her 100th birthday, 'Chislehurst has not changed very much, the place is very much the same on the whole, the Commons prevents it from changing too much.'

Mabel went to Girton in 1891 but is listed as without occupation on the 1901 census, and died of emphysema in 1955, aged 83, as a spinster of independent means. She had moved to Ormestead, The Meadow, after Ethel died in 1938. There was apparently no family left to attend to her, and she was buried by undertakers H. A. Bulley. She left an estate of £11,000 in probate to Martins Bank.

Just when I thought that was the end of the story, a tiny fact threw up a perverse twist in this charming family's tale. Frederick Edmeston, he of the Black Forest incident, died, just one year after his mother, in 1935. Always an interesting character, as I knew his children were born in Japan, he became particularly fascinating when I spotted he had died on a tennis court in Ireland! I couldn't let this go. Crockford's Clerical Directory revealed much of his curriculum vitae. He had attended Dulwich College as a boy, and went to Trinity College, Oxford in 1885, gaining an MA in history. He went to Tokyo as a missionary in 1886, returning in 1888. He married Edith Susan Wood in 1892 at St Martin-in-the-Fields. The couple returned to Japan, to Yokohama, where Evelyn was born in 1893. A second daughter, Audrey, was born in Canterbury in 1896. Frederick then became Vicar of Whittlesey, near Ely in Cambridgeshire, before becoming a Chaplain at Wiesbaden, Germany, in 1917. What kind of war must he have had, stationed in enemy country? He finally came back to England to become Vicar of St Etheldreda with St Clement, Fulham. Frederick retired at the end of 1928. Then came the jolt: he died at his son's in Ireland but was buried at Putney Vale. I didn't even know he had a son, nor that there was a Freese grandson, since there was no mention of any grandchildren in Octavia's obituary.

To obtain a certain closure on Frederick, I had to learn more about this 'son'. Not easy, as he was never listed on any census, so I had no name or date of birth to go on. I went back to his mother, Edith Wood, and – bingo! – I found an hilarious story which may have horrified old Octavia, a story of name-changing to inherit a fortune, but also dissipation of that fortune. That's probably why there had been no mention of her grandson, who turns out to be the wonderfully-named British diplomat Harold Wilfred Armine Freese-Pennefather!

Armine, as he was known, had been born in 1907, so I would only have found him on a 1911 census, but by that time Frederick and family were in Germany, so avoided my discovery! His mother was from the Pennefather family of Rathsallagh, Ireland. Her brother, another Fred, a staunch Unionist, died without issue and Armine was next in succession to the Irish estate in County Wicklow. He assumed his additional surname of Pennefather by deed poll in 1922. Yet he was to be largely an absentee landlord. After an education at Eton and Balliol College, Oxford, Armine entered the diplomatic service in 1930 and started a four year contract as third secretary to the British Embassy in Washington. So he would have been abroad when his grandmother died. I'm still surprised the Kentish Times reporter didn't comment on Octavia's illustrious grandson; I wonder if relations were strained?

According to The Family History pages relating to the Pennefathers, the estate in Ireland kept the Freeses' London household in fruit and vegetables, with peaches being personally bottled by the estate manager's wife. Armine must have spent some time in Ireland, though, as his father died there on 22 August 1935, on that tennis court!

Following his father's death, Armine was transferred to the British Embassy in Buenos Aires, where he remained until 1938. At the outbreak of the Second World War, he was second in command in Oslo, but relocated to Baghdad following the Nazi invasion of Norway. He served in London from 1944 to 1949 and married just before Christmas 1949. It would seem that Armine was a sometime resident of Rathsallagh; perhaps he took his new bride to see his inherited pad. A neighbour recalls how the flourishing diplomat could – in a move that would surely have caused his Tractarian grandparents to spin in their graves – spend money left, right and centre, with polo ponies, badminton halls and squash courts on the estate. Armine's diplomatic career continued after his marriage, with appointments to the British Consuls in Burma, Rabat and Morocco. His daughter, Susan, born in 1953, went on to marry show-jumper Eddie Macken. Armine lived until 1961, when he was British Ambassador to Luxembourg. The Pennefather family sold the estates to their tenants in the wake of Irish Independence. The grand house still remains, declared Irish Country House of the year in 2000.

Christ Church today

8. Christ Church

1872 - 1900
Reverend William Fleming: The Search for a Parsonage

William Fleming was a distinctive figure in the early life of the road but he did give me some orienteering challenges! In trying to unravel his accommodation and that of the Christ Church parsonage, I have had had many happy conversations with church archivist Christopher Scott. Chris has updated the history of Christ Church and produced a comprehensive booklet on the church and its history. In anticipation of its publication, we exchanged notes, indulging ourselves in that glorious occupation of double-checking facts and data against census, church archives and historic documents in our possession. It took a phone call from Chris's wife, asking if he was ever heading home, to makes us realise we had been discussing Fleming, the itinerant minister, for well over three hours!

William Fleming was from Ennis Clare in Ireland and it's rather delightful to read his letters to his mother, addressed 'Now, darling Mammy'. His professional life had actually begun in the army and he served in the Boer War. He was with the 45th (Nottinghamshire) Regiment of Foot from 1845 to 1864, and was present at the Battle of Boemplats. He was awarded the Kaffir War medal. He wrote, 'You cannot think how happy I am to find that I am really at last a soldier and not playing at them'. William's regiment is commemorated in stained glass in the north transept at Christ Church. It was given, along with the brass lectern, by grateful parishioners, no doubt many of them residents of the road, for his 28 year ministry.

On leaving the army, William went to Cambridge, having won a scholarship to St Catharine's College. He graduated with a First in Law. He was ordained in 1857 in Chichester, moving on to Brighton before becoming junior chaplain to the Home and Colonial Institute. He was nominated by the trustees of Christ Church to become their vicar in 1872, having come from a parish in Crouch End; he was to be the incumbent until his death. In 1880, he also became secretary of the London Society for the Promotion of Christianity among the Jews, an interesting forerunner to a later role in the life of the church.

But a paragraph from his obituary, recorded in the St Nicholas parish magazine of 1900, gives the most tantalising comment as to his character: 'Mr Fleming's views in religious matters were of one particular line, in which his earnestness and sincerity of purpose were much appreciated by those who knew him as a clergyman, and personally. It was often regretted that he did not feel disposed or able to mix with others of his clerical neighbours, no doubt to a mutual loss, when greater freedom of intercourse would have been beneficial to all.' So, was he an independent spirit, a loner or a pompous, overbearing type, someone who did things his way? I can't be certain, but he doesn't seem to have been the most congenial man in the neighbourhood, going by this tacit note.

The whole idea of Christ Church was conceived in the sitting room of Mr Thomas Archibald of Inglewood. The inaugural committee included one Mr W.R.Winch, a tea trader who lived at Hillside in Lubbock Road. Inglewood is now the sixth form centre at Bullers Wood School on Chislehurst Road, and from the windows of the school you can see the tower of Christ Church. The land for the church was donated by the now familiar property developer Nathaniel Strode. In the autumn of 1870 Strode's offer of land was accepted and the site of the church, but not the surrounding area, became consecrated land. Inside the outer porch is a commemorative plaque to Nathaniel Strode, and I was pleased to show that to Nat's great grandson, Richard, in 2014.

Christ Church was built within the parish of St Nicholas, and was very much the brainchild of Evangelical churchgoers, namely Lord Sydney and

Christ Church with spire, 1872

Frederick Edlmann, who were disturbed by Canon Murray's high church rituals at St Nicholas parish church. Lord Sydney laid the foundation stone on 10 June 1871, standing in for his wife, who was indisposed with a cold. The ceremony of consecration on Monday, 29 July was performed by the Archbishop of Canterbury in the 'presence of a large number of gentry of the district'. A procession of about a dozen clergy from the diocese was formed and, perhaps in the spirit of co-operation, Canon Murray was in attendance. It poured with rain on the day, but that didn't stop the enjoyment of 'refreshments of an abundant character' in a spacious marquee at Inglewood.

On 1 June 1871, the Bromley Record reported preparations going on for the building of the new church on the side of the hill in Camden Park, and in view of the existence of caves in the vicinity, warned the builders 'to ascertain that they are not undermined lest some fine morning when the spire is nearly finished, the workmen may come and find the top of it just peeping out of the ground'!

The building has clearly survived. It is an impressive and attractive church of Kentish rag stone designed by architects Habershon and Pite, of Bloomsbury. The original spire only lasted six years, not due to any landslip or cowboy building, but more through an incredible lack of vision (easy to say with hindsight). The original church was simply too small, designed to

Christ Church with tower, 1880

Rev, William Fkeming

seat 500, and a further 200 were soon needed.

The extension project, which resulted in changing the spire to a tower, is a perfect reflection of the rapid development that was going on in Chislehurst (and many other London suburbs) at the time. The arrival of the railway in 1865 enabled merchants and professionals to commute easily to work in London. The resulting building boom was exactly what Nathaniel Strode had banked on changing Chislehurst beyond recognition, so how could the church commissioners and architects not have foreseen this development? Fleming, addressing a meeting in Christ Church School Room in Old Hill in 1877, said that since the church had opened, 28 houses and a number of cottages had been built in the immediate vicinity of the church, and about a hundred new members had joined in the previous year. The decision to enlarge the church, seconded by Mr Tiarks, was carried unanimously.

The cost of the building at the outset was in the region of £5,000. It was also considered desirable to secure a home for Rev. Fleming, but funds were short by some £3,000, and so began the story of what can only be described as a 'wandering minister'. Rev. Fleming was to live at four different addresses in the road during his ministry; that took quite a lot of map-reading and interpretation, I can tell you!

The accommodation for this minister, his wife Anna – 12 years his senior, from Waterford in Ireland, the daughter of a naval officer – and her sister should rightly be described as a parsonage. Vicarage or rectory are terms attached to a parish, whereas Christ Church was not a separate parish in 1872. The 1871 census reports Rev. and Mrs Fleming residing in Crouch End with Anna's sister and William's mother. The 1881 census sees them in Chislehurst, but it's frustrating: they are listed as being at Camden Park – this is potentially Lubbock Road, as that is listed at the top of the page and Ravensbrook is the neighbouring property – but the evidence falls short of being explicit. The 1887 street directory lists Fleming as living at Bankside, referred to as 'Camden Parsonage', between Kincraig and Ravensbrook (now Burlington Lodge), which is more satisfactory in pinning down the actual house. From 1888 to 1890, he seems to have been at Abbey Lodge, and from 1891 to 1893 he is residing at Hillside, opposite Abbey Lodge. (Hillside was demolished around 1937, as my sepia photograph from that era shows a barren plot). All of this intrigues me and is not resolved in my mind. Abbey Lodge and Hillside were huge family houses, not the sort of house that a church minister could afford, or that just three people with a small staff would need. Moreover, why did they have to move so often? A distant employer and the vagaries of renting, possibly. His poor aged wife, having to manage all that moving about, albeit just along the road! Anna predeceased William; she is listed on the 1891 census and died in April 1897, aged 80. Her final change of address came in 1894, when the Flemings moved into Beechcroft, the house on the same side of the road as the church.

Beechcroft is now the site of Lubbock Court. I have seen a sad photograph of the original house being demolished, and layout plans for the new property. It was a sign of the times that old houses were becoming uneconomic to run, draughty and unwelcoming, perhaps. The only original house in this section of Lubbock Road is Bishopsdown, formerly Bankside. I haven't found a story connected with this particular old house, other than the achievement of a former, more recent occupant being awarded the Templeton Prize for Progress in Religion. Michael Bordeaux, founder of Keston College in England, was awarded this prize in 1984.

At last, Christ Church had seemingly found a permanent home for its incumbent. However, I knew from the deeds of my own home that half of my house had in 1957 been used 'for a parsonage house' and was to remain so until 1966. I searched for a while for a name for my house, rather than simply calling it number 68; it was far too beautiful not to have a name. The deeds specifically precluded me from using the title 'The Old Rectory' or 'Parsonage'. In the end, I settled on Brackens, another name within the property's complicated paperwork and added, in brackets, formerly 'The Rookery', for the avoidance of any doubt and – of course – as an aide to future historians!

The new vicarage was finally built at 62 Lubbock Road. It only took ninety-four years, but I suppose in historic terms that's small beer!

Back in 1900, and on the urgent advice of his brother, widower Fleming went to London for medical advice and was treated for some length of time. He made it known that he wished to return home to his friends in Chislehurst, but he had a relapse and died on 20 May 1900. His brother, Canon James Fleming, conducted his funeral at Christ Church, and William was interred alongside his mother and wife at Kensal Green Cemetery. This happened to be on Ascension Day and it was noted in other church records that many local clergy were therefore unable to attend the service; or was that a convenient diversion, allowing them a reason not to attend the funeral of an awkward man?

9. Ravensbrook

1873 - 1895
Reverend John Macduff: A Million Book Sales

Having already learned about the spiritual leanings of Octavia Freese and Charles Janson, I was beginning to think the road had some sort of stream of holy water running through it. I wasn't remotely surprised, therefore, to discover the story of more reverends in the road. The lives of John Ross Macduff, DDiv, and the Reverend William Wight, go hand in hand as the discovery of the autobiography of the one led to the whimsical story of the other. Rev. John Ross Macduff lived at Ravensbrook, on the site of what is now Burlington Court. A chance discussion about trees with my friend from neighbouring Ross Court confirmed the setting and led us on an environmentally-inspired expedition into communal gardens; we were probably trespassing, but I hope we will be forgiven.

There are several short references to this John Ross via Google, and I might have overlooked him as a worthy subject for further research as,

Ravensbrook, built 1873

initially, his story seemed rather dry and distant. A Scottish Presbyterian minister, educated in Edinburgh, who worked in Glasgow and then retired to Chislehurst. What would a devoted Scot be doing here in Kent? Then I came across a picture of the bearded man, very dour and certainly distinctive. Hymnary.org (yes, there is such a site) gave more detail, which drew me in.

The second son of Alexander Macduff, of Bonhard, near Perth, was born on 23 May 1818. After studying at the University of Edinburgh, he became, in 1842, parish minister of Kettins, Forfarshire; in 1849 parish minister of St Madoes, Perthshire; and in 1855 the same of a new church in Sandyford, Glasgow. In 1857, the general assembly appointed him to its Hymnal Committee. His 31 hymns appeared in his book Altar Stones, and were also included with his later poems in The Gates of Praise. I can't say I recognise any of the titles, but I can feel his high Victorian spiritual passion in 'Eternal Rock, to thee I flee' and 'He who on the accursed tree'. I wonder if he knew Octavia Freese's dad?

My researcher's nose sniffed more interest when the biographical note stated that he received his Doctorate of Divinity from the University of Glasgow in 1862 and simultaneously from New York University. Why was that; why were the Americans interested? His digitised autobiography revealed the answer. His books attained a circulation in America of three million, and many were translated into other languages! Tales of the Warrior King: The Life and Times of David, the King of Israel was described by The Scotsman as 'a volume written in spirited style, and with a proper appreciation of the opportunities which its subject affords of improving the tale'... was our JR prone to hyperbole? Along with his books on teaching, he wrote words of comfort for the hours of sorrow. 'Among the many books of comfort for Christian mourners we do not know a better than this', wrote The Daily Mail of Pillars in the Night. I looked on Amazon and bought myself a copy of The Bow in the Cloud for £1.99. A beautiful little book, smelling of mothballs, which a Jane H. Patterson had given to Mr and Mrs Furey in January 1891, inscribed 'with love and sorrowing sympathy'. I hope it brought the required solace to the recipients.

As I mentioned earlier, the internet also led me to the 195 pages of JR's autobiography, edited by his daughter Annie. This weighty tome does give some insights into our distinctive Doctor who made his fortune out of sorrow. He wrote the work having been urged to do so by friends; he describes himself as sitting in his summer- house, 'weakened by an exhausting illness of many months and having no love of self laudations'.

His first wife, Anne Seton, had died, aged just 20 years old, in 1846; he was a widower at just twenty-eight. No wonder he knew how to write about grief.

At St Madoes, the idea struck him that 'it would be a pleasant thing to send to the head of each family in my former parish some printed souvenir in the form of a tract or small book. I thought it might be well to cast the same in the shape of a few words for daily reading. This was the origin of The Faithful Promiser, the speedy and almost immediate sale of which, extending to hundreds of thousands almost frightened me.' As a result, he received a request from Mr Nisbet of Berners Street, London, a well-known religious publisher, for more works. The Morning and Night Watches, which next went to press, enjoyed a circulation of half a million.

He married a second time, Louisa Stephen, in 1849, a thirty-eight year union which he says 'greatly contributed to the serenity in my life'. He describes her thus: 'Doing justly; loving mercy; walking humbly. Even in my literary work I reliably leant on her taste and accuracy'. Louisa was a Londoner, her father a close intimate of General Lawrence of India.

In 1857, his son (from his first marriage) died very suddenly; he was only twelve and 'full of promise'. The outcome of this bereavement was the book I now have in my possession, The Bow in the Cloud. JR's autobiography clearly is true to his desire not to dwell on himself; there are fewer than four lines devoted to the death of his child and there is no reference whatsoever to the birth of his daughter in 1850. Perhaps Annie edited herself out of his autobiography!

In 1867, he was invited to deliver a speech in Glasgow City Hall in honour of Dr Livingstone. He received the following day a copy of Livingstone's own book, personally inscribed with his 'kindest salutations'. It is interesting to note, given his later abode, that in that in 1870 he commented on his colleagues reading in the newspapers of the surrender of Napoleon III and his army at Sedan, on the same day as his own resignation was tendered. He had decided, given the 'undiminished success of authorship', to devote himself in the future to the 'engagements of the press'.

At this point, the digital autobiography took me by surprise. There were some unexplained single lines with quotes by Robert Murray Esq. I realised there were photographs in the original that had not been transferred to the digital text. My excitement was unbounded; I found the book for sale via my account at Amazon. There were indeed photographs of the house, garden and study. This being a print on demand copy, they are very poor reproductions, but still are precious images.

He 'was resolved to buy a piece of ground and build a small house. It must for many reasons be close to London, with its ever throbbing arteries of life. There must be some large trees. If possible, undulating ground, or better, a defunct quarry – and rarer still, in Kentish soil, a running stream. Quite incredibly (and I'm beginning to feel shades of Octavia Freese's telepathic thoughts, here), all these conditions, right down to the disused chalk quarry, were satisfied in Lubbock Road. Full instructions were given to a clever architect (sadly un-named) who created a pretty and aesthetic dwelling in the early Tudor style. During the building phase, JR obtained by the courtesy of his freeholder, the one and only Nathaniel Strode, a private entrance to see the Emperor Napoleon III lying in state in the temporary Chapelle Ardente. 'The olive countenance, the blazing candles and the low muttered prayers of the priests formed an impression never to be forgotten'.

JR also notes that there was a church – Christ Church – 'just being completed within gunshot, but whose ecclesiastical proclivities he did not know'. The day on which Strode's 'worthy and hearty' bailiff (Adcock?) came in to measure off the freehold, JR asked him, 'what party does the church with a spire [this was before the tower] belong to'? The bailiff's answer was brief, instantaneous, significant: 'it's the lowest of the low'. It was to become JR's place of worship for the years to come, and has an internal stained-glass window to his memory.

He and his family lived at Norwood whilst the new house was being built, and moved into Ravensbrook in June 1873. It became a 'very happy residence'. The complete quiet, the kindness of new neighbours, the easy access to town and many other desirable features were appreciated. He describes the grounds as 'limited', 'hardly more than two acres', but picturesque. He enjoyed laying out the gardens and planted his special favourites, conifers and weeping trees. The latter was quite a hobby. A clever lady friend suggested calling the house' Niobe Lodge' – Niobe is the Greek goddess who weeps for her children. Visits to Switzerland and the Riviera yielded valuable cuttings which have now transformed themselves. This is how I have been able to absolutely confirm the location of Ravensbrook. Chatting over an ever-ready cup of coffee with a friend, we were discussing gardens and arboriculture, as we so regularly do!! She mentioned in passing that contractors for the flats next to her were amazed by the beauty of one particular specimen – a weeping beech! Some months later, she took me

Rev. John Ross Macduff

Louisa Macduff and daughter Annie

The weeping beech at Ravensbrook

Memorial window at Christ Church to John Ross Macduff
See detail below

Born in Scotland, 1818

Died at Chislehurst, 1895

on a spur of the moment tour; the trees are beautiful to behold: a huge redwood and at least two weeping beeches. It was a wonderful moment of confirmation.

In 1888, on 4 January, Louisa died. They had been married 38 years. The fever she had while in Rome, fifteen years before, had returned and, after weeks of great suffering, she had a heart attack. Their daughter tended her, rejecting all proposals to have a trained nurse. JR describes his daughter has having 'tender, loving, dutiful ways by word and deed with a devotion in which self had no consideration, much, natural to a young life, has been cheerfully and resolutely surrendered for our sake'. Annie suffered 'acute prostration', and her mother's grave was a thing of rare beauty, a marble tombstone and marble kerb, with ever-fresh flowers. Apparently, of all the graves in Chislehurst churchyard, none was so beautifully tended; now, sadly, it is broken in two.

JR himself had paroxysmal neuralgia; every nerve at the back of head and neck was a chord of agony, great and persistent. Injections of morphine dulled the pain for a little and induced a troubled sleep, but he died on 30 April 1895, aged 77.

Annie lived for a further thirty-four years, and died a spinster, aged 79, in the Priory, Roehampton.

1874
Hannah Broomfield: Loyal Servant

The stories I have discovered have been about the fortunate, those who left a distinctive footprint, so readily traceable in this technological age. I was delighted, therefore, to find this short description of a young woman, servant to John Ross Macduff.

Hannah was a domestic servant, one of many, no doubt, who came to work for the prosperous middle classes in Chislehurst as she did, in January 1874. Her story is brief and rather pathetic, but is admirably told by her master, Dr Macduff himself, and may very well not be that unusual.

She was born in Church Staunton, Honiton, Devon. Her father had died when she was five, and she was sole carer to her aging mother. After leaving home to go into service, Hannah used to send sovereigns back home for her mother. She had a happy and affectionate childhood; her mother apparently earned her keep gathering stones in the fields. Hannah went to Sunday school, sat on her father's grave reading her bible, and she sang hymns frequently around the house, especially on Sundays, her favourite being 'Abide With Me'.

Macduff writes: 'Her pronunciation was devoid of provincialism, she was a humble, hard-working house maid. She waited at table, received and admitted visitors; evidently on an erroneous estimate of propriety, she assumed a gravity which was not her usual demeanour'.

Tragically, she died at the age of just 26. Hannah had pleurisy; 'she became passive and dull instead of vivacious. She became visibly less able to do the household work, accomplished hitherto with such satisfaction. She struggled on until the lurking disease compelled her to give up. Throughout her illness there was distressing difficulty breathing and exceptional periods of painlessness. The day before she died she announced her engagement to the young gardener, George. She asked for her favourite little dog, who jumped on her bed. With strange instinct the animal seemed to droop during her illness, he usually resented the intrusion of a single stranger into the house but he was silent when many strange feet were conveying her down stairs for her last journey'.

Macduff refers to choosing a grave spot at St Nicholas churchyard and being cheered by the sound of the pealing bells. George brought snowdrops and primroses from the dell near the Kyd hearing both 'near and distant' church bells. The tolling of the village bell met the bearers of the dead through the picturesque lych gate, the sun slowly westering behind old elm trees and gilding the tiles of the neighbouring chapel under whose modest roof repose the remains of the illustrious Imperial exile'. It was exactly a year since the death of Napoleon III.

A sorry story, but one that bears telling. Servants were very much part of the whole family and, as far as I'm concerned, they are equally worthy of notes on these pages.

10. The Arab's Tent

1874 - 1884
Reverend William Wight: Dreams of a Domestic Nature

Quirky houses are always intriguing. The Arab's Tent is the original name of the large house situated behind Christ Church. It is technically not even in Lubbock Road, but so many people wonder about this magnificent pile and its curious original name that I have to include it in the history of the road. It was clearly part of the Camden Park Estate developed by Strode, and for that reason alone I feel justified in its inclusion. More truthfully, you just can't miss out on this tale of would-be philanthropy and a family legal battle over the sanity of a potential benefactor.

The house name appears on the 1893 indenture of Camden Park, and the Rev. William Wight is listed in the Kelly's Directories as the owner from 1878. The plot of land was originally purchased for development from Strode in 1874, by his land agent Frederick Adcock, but whatever Adcock did with the land, Wight was the first resident. When I researched Wight, I just knew he was going to be a distinctive character, possibly a man with a

The Arab's Tent - Stowcroft, c.1920

fortune, or at least so he believed. In the 1891 census, he describes himself as a vicar of 'no souls'. His life in Chislehurst was one of retirement. Clear eccentricities emerged as I delved a little deeper; he was definitely worthy of further investigation. I knew I was onto a good thing when I came across a brilliant description of Wight's character in the autobiography of his neighbour, Dr Macduff. Then I struck gold with a phone call to the charming people of the Harbury Community Library in Warwickshire!

I found Wight's alumni record from Corpus Christi, Cambridge, which showed he had come to Chislehurst from his last position as vicar of Harbury. I googled 'Harbury' and found a reference to Wight School, which opened in 1856, Wight had been instrumental in starting fund raising for the building. Above the door of the school was an inscription that bears his name to this day. The school is now a library run by a charity, with volunteers offering tea and cake and the internet, as well as books. Tantalisingly, on their website was a presentation entitled 'the History of the Wight School Building', but, frustratingly, the presentation was 'in preparation'. Not one to let those words be a barrier, I hovered over the telephone number for a couple of minutes, then, taking a deep breath, I dialled the number. That day's volunteer, John Eld, was delightful and an exceptionally helpful chap. He suggested I speak to his fellow villager John Stringer, who was about to go to press with the History that I was after. I was even given a direct telephone number and told to blame the first John if I was disturbing the second one.

Wonderfully, I got an immediate response; John Two – John Springer – was interested in my findings from Macduff and, teasingly, asked me if I wanted to see a photograph. Did I ever?! What a 'history high' to receive a photo, however hazy, of 'The Arab' himself. This John was generous enough to share his History with me: *1852-1865: William Wight, the Model Minister*.

I learned that William was a practical Christian, temperance advocate and humanitarian. He had a lifelong enthusiasm for temperance and the positive social effects of abstinence. He wanted to found an ideal society in a teetotal village; Harbury became the chosen setting. His aim was to improve the condition of the villagers, to ensure that they had sound moral character and that they did not drink or smoke. In 1853, he helped establish the 'Harbury Cottage Improvement Garden and Floricultural Association', which was aimed at 'improved dwellings for the working classes and securing greater attendance to cleanliness and to sanitary principles'. A Moral Police patrolled the village between nine and twelve at night to 'visit places of resort and observe the state of the parish'. Wight organised evening classes on three nights of the week and a Model Library of three hundred volumes, but with 'no works of fiction or of questionable character'. I'm so glad I didn't live there!

Wight's School was set up to educate the village children and 'bring them up in the Christian Spirit'. The school attempted to 'combine industrial training with the intellectual course of instruction to prepare the children for the duties of public and private life and to qualify some for the office of teachers and other employment and some for domestic service'. This instruction in household duties and cleanliness was obviously merely a precursor to the ultimate ambition revealed in his will.

Wight left the living of Harbury in 1865, and there is a record of his living in Chislehurst from 1878 at the house that is now called Stowcroft, although, as I discovered, Wight named it 'The Arab's Tent'. Knowing of Wight's ideals of creating a model and sober society, I am left wondering whether he was behind the opening of the temperance Coffee Tavern on Chislehurst High Street. The building is still there today, and high up in the gable next to the old police station, you might just make out the words Coffee Tavern, carved on a stone tablet. There were public baths in the basement, and a club room with a billiard table, bagatelle and chess boards. The building served only non-alcoholic refreshments. Opened in 1881, it closed a few years later, owing to the management committee's refusing to permit Sunday opening.

The reminiscences of Dr Macduff are so revealing, and I was glad to be able to share these with John Springer, in return for his History. Together, they complete the picture of this colourful character. Macduff recalls his late friend as 'kind, sympathetic and hospitable, despite very pronounced eccentricities, which all of his acquaintances understood, excused and condoned'. Macduff tells us that Wight had been a great traveller, specifically in Egypt, Arabia and Syria, which 'had impelled him, by force of the same eccentricities, to give his spacious house the name 'The Arab's Tent'. The penalty for which indiscretion, he had, of course himself to pay, by being called 'The Arab'.' Never one to be without an opinion, Wight expressed his views on the Russo-Turkish War of 1877-8, publishing *Cross and Crescent: A Word for the Mohammedan in the Present War*. It was subtitled: With Reminiscences of Travel in Mohammedan Countries. On the roofline of Stowcroft today is a cross and crescent weather vane.

Wight had a 'singular and fortunate aptitude for gathering many nice, and some distinguished, people around him. Literary, artistic, secular and sacred. He could even bag an eastern Patriarch, or a Bishop of Jerusalem, or a home church dignitary, or a Times correspondent, or such a celebrity as Mr Christian Rassam an archaeologist in Iraq, whom he brought to spend a pleasant evening at Ravensbrook'.

'The Arab' died at home in Chislehurst in October 1884, and the alumni record from Cambridge has the intriguing addition that Wight left nearly all his property – about £10,000 – in trust to found Wight's College of Social and Domestic Science for Ladies. Given all that I had learned from John Stringer in Harbury, that wish was entirely in keeping with the aims and ideals with which Wight had led his life. But then the report goes on to say that the trusts were declared null and void under the Mortmain Acts. These are statutes designed to prevent land from being perpetually possessed or controlled by religious corporations. A clever use of legalities by the family, one suspects.

Wight's incredible, if tortuous to read, will was contested by his New Zealander heir, on the grounds of Wight's insanity. The lineage of this New Zealand heir has proven impossible to trace. William was a widower but his wife's name has not been determined. He left money to Miss Helen Wight of Clapham and Mrs Adamson of Devonshire Hill, Hampstead... a sister, maybe? Probate was granted to his brother, Edward Wight of Clapham; Helen was his daughter, so maybe it was she who emigrated to New Zealand. There is a report in New Zealand's Timaru Herald, in January 1889, of the case heard by Mr Justice Chitty. I got hold of the will and Wight's death certificate. He died of 'consolidation of the left lung'; he had been suffering for the last four months and was 'exhausted'. Curiously, the will, drawn up in June 1884, before the onset of the pneumonia that killed him, was signed off at University College Hospital. Had he been admitted for another medical investigation? He was never proved to be insane but the will was still declared void. Overall, the case took five years to settle, and Justice Chitty finally made an order giving specific directions as to the distribution of the property among the next of kin.

The will is a masterpiece of verbosity and sincere intent. The Reverend owned houses both in Chislehurst and Cheltenham, along with French and Spanish government bonds, from the sale of which he expected to raise £1,000. He anticipated that the Chislehurst house be let furnished but his books, coins and foreign curiosities be sold to raise a further £10,000.

Rev. William Wight

His desire was for another house to be built on the land at Chislehurst, of 'ornamental but useful style'! The house was to be built between the existing structure and the church path, and the two houses were to be connected by a pretty glazed arcade. It seems the idea for the glazed link building at Christ Church was stolen from him! These two houses were to found the aforementioned Wight's College to train ladies for the important duties of wife, mistress and housekeeper, to provide a wholesome protest against the present defective training of ladies. Apparently, he felt the training at the time was wholly defective and the framework of society was more or less affected by it. 'The incompetent mistress makes bad servants and bad servants make bad wives and bad wives through their ignorance, idleness and extravagance make bad homes and bad homes drive men to ruin and taint national life'. Please note: I am quoting verbatim from the vicar himself.

The rules of the College were set out in his will, too; he had clearly put a lot of thought into it and of course had had previous experience from his school in Harbury. 'To escape the enervating atmosphere of gas-heated rooms at night and the foul air of bedrooms in the morning the inmates [bad choice of words!] shall leave their rooms no later than 6 in the summer and 7 in the winter, retiring no later than 9 in winter and half past in summer. A sponge bath shall be provided and used in each room. No bedroom to be left in the morning until the bedclothes have been well stripped and windows partially opened top and bottom. [Today's teenagers, take note!] There shall be family devotions night and morning with singing and music, a verse of appointed scripture shall be read by the ladies in rotation under the direction of the lady supervisor'. They would receive three not four wholesome meals a day and, naturally, no intoxicating drinks would be used at the College.

The ladies were to 'cultivate elegant neatness of dress'. Cards, dancing and 'trashy novels' were to be excluded, but healthy games such as tennis were to be encouraged; chess and bagatelle was acceptable in the winter. There would be quarterly meetings of the board of governors, and up to 12 Governors could be paid travelling expenses of two guineas. 'Conversaziones' were to be held with refreshments and 'single gentlemen' invited. Victorian Tinder, eh? At these events, the last chapter of Proverbs was to be read by a clergyman of the Church of England. I wonder if he had Macduff in mind for that job?

No lady was to remain permanently in the College; most periods of residence were to be from 12 to 18 months. At annual prize giving, 'useful articles of domestic service such as silver teapots' were to be awarded, in three degrees of merit, and each engraved 'Wight's College of Social and Domestic Service'. He obviously expected his brand of colleges to expand, as he intended this college to be self-supporting and 'any surplus of funds to go to branch colleges'. However, the will was declared void and the College was never established; thus the ladies of Chislehurst were denied their sponge baths and male company.

In actual fact, the probate sum achieved from his personal estate was £4,088. A significant enough sum, but not possibly the fortune the family was expecting; perhaps 'they' wanted the cash from the sale of his house as well, and that's why the will was contested. I suppose New Zealand is rather too far away from which to successfully manage an educational establishment!

William had also clearly prescribed what should happen 'in the event of my dying in England'. 'My corpse may lie in my own grounds under the bank immediately in front of the drawing room window leading to the terrace near where my dog "Friend" lies'. He wanted a 'small but substantial ornamental mausoleum to be erected with shelves on each side for the reception of the bodies of the Ladies Superior and Lady Matrons who may wish to be there'. Brompton Cemetery was to suggest a model for the mausoleum but he wanted the door opening into the mausoleum to be partially glazed and protected by bronze lattice. His epitaph was to read: 'No man liveth to himself, give an account of thy stewardship, whatever thy hand findeth to do, do it, with thy might'. Additionally, he wanted another memorial inscribed for his Labrador: 'Friend lies here, at the feet of his attached and sorrowing master. Friend was friendly with all and all were friendly with Friend'.

Despite his request, Wight is buried in St Nicholas churchyard. Dr Macduff wrote the words engraved on his headstone: 'Rev. William Wight formerly Vicar of Harbury, Warwickshire, lately resident in Lower Camden, Chislehurst. Obit. 16 Oct 1884 Obdormivit in Christo.' He was 74 years old. I don't think Canon Murray would have set the precedent of allowing a dog to be buried in his hallowed ground, so I suspect the remains of the devoted creature are somewhere deep in the grounds of Stowcroft, and that the current owners may be somewhat relieved not to have an ornate mausoleum in their garden.

But are we richer, or the poorer, for not having a domestic science college in the locality, where women can be taught 'to be something more useful and noble than a pretty doll, a butterfly or a plaything for their husband'? You decide! Eccentric he certainly was, but his heart was in a good place!

As far as I can determine, the next owner of the house, Mr G Manger, retained the name, and it was Miss Harriett de Quincey – living on her own means and indeed alone, with just two servants in 1911: something of a Miss Havisham- like character, perhaps – who first used the name 'Stowcroft'. The census reveals that the house had 30 rooms: plenty of space for a Domestic Science College, in fact!

Camden Lodge, 70 Lubbock Road

11. Camden Lodge

1884 -1930
The Wood Family: The House with an Organ Chamber

Nathaniel Strode began parcelling up the land on the corner of Lubbock Road and Old Hill in 1884 so that it could be sold for building. It was bought by builders Frederick and William John Adcock from Dover. The indenture which records the legalities of the sale makes great reading: 'The said William John Adcock shall not at any time hereafter erect or suffer to be erected upon the said land any building whatsoever except detached private dwelling house of not less value than £800 exclusive of stabling, gardener's lodges, greenhouses, summerhouses or suitable outbuildings to such dwellinghouses or any of them without consent from the said Nathaniel William John Strode......and shall not permit any premises or any part thereof in such a manner as to be a nuisance or annoyance to the said Nathaniel William John Strode.' This purchase may have been even more Machiavellian than it may first appear. Frederick Adcock was in business with Strode; he later became his land agent and, indeed, following Strode's death, Adcock married Nat's widow, Eleanor!

The original house on this plot still exists, but is split into flats from basement to attic. The census of 1891 is the first to identify the occupants, and it clearly identifies Peter Frederick Wood as living at Camden Lodge. How very aspirational, to call a substantial four-storey house a 'lodge'!

Researching the Wood family was probably my most satisfying experience of this whole journey of discovery into the 'lives of my road'. They were of great fortune and earned distinction that has been recorded for posterity. The Wood family had been investigated by a living relative on Ancestry, and 'Bex' was the first contributor I ever made contact with. I'm not sure I would have bothered to write, had it not been for a geographical error on the public family tree. Bex had been researching the life of her deceased great-grandfather, Wilfred Burton Wood. Her family tree stated that he was born at Camden Lodge, Surrey. Being something of a pedant, I sent a note, saying was she sure it was Surrey, as I felt sure it was my neighbouring property here in Chislehurst, Kent. I added that the house was still standing and that I could show her the house if she was interested.

It was a heart-palpitating moment when a message dropped into my inbox, saying that the family certainly lived at Camden Lodge, as Emily,

Wilfred's mother, had a short book written about her life as a Wesleyan teacher, and the book had photos of the house which were taken at the turn of the century. To a researcher, the words, 'book' and 'photographs' in the same sentence give cause for hysterical excitement. They also give rise to another purchase from Amazon. A tatty little book, *A Life's Work Well Done: A Memorial Sketch of Mrs Emily Wood*, arrived three days later, and with literally trembling hands, I opened the delicate pages to reveal a photograph of Camden Lodge c.1886. Furthermore, there was an additional photograph of 'The Organ Chamber'!

Unfortunately, the frontispiece, which contained a picture of Emily herself, was missing, but there was a picture of her headstone in Southport, giving the date of her death as 23 July 1904, at Llanfairfechan, Wales. The little book reveals why she was in Wales, making many references to Emily's poor health. Her death certificate, which I ordered, revealed the full extent of her illness: chronic Bright's disease, of the kidneys. The symptoms were severe back pain, vomiting, fever, severely restricted breathing and acute inflammation, even of the face. Treatment then would have involved blood-letting, warm baths, diuretics and laxatives.

Bex had also referred in her message to the untimely death of Peter Norris Wood, the eldest son, in Mesopotamia in the First World War.

Peter's story is one of real dedication and service. I already knew of some of the circumstances, from the intensely written story of all the Chislehurst war dead, *For King and Country*, by Yvonne Auld. I had contacted Yvonne when I first read her book and told her about my research. She was quick to tell me more, about the beautiful memorial to Peter in the Methodist Church on Prince Imperial Road, as well as the memorial to the survivors of the War, his brothers, Wilfred Burton and Gordon Frederick. Barely containing my excitement, I got back in touch with Bex and offered to show her the house and the memorials. It was a genuine thrill when she responded, asking if her grandmother could join us on the visit, and see the house where her father grew up. This was exciting for me, but intensely moving for the real people of this story. I think at this point I wondered if I was intruding, poking my nose into other people's lives where I really had no business being.

Fortunately, we had the most touching afternoon together. On a bright, sunny September afternoon, the Lewis family, Wood descendants on the distaff side, came for tea, along with Yvonne. What a splendid occasion! I met Becky, a history student, her father and her Grandmother – who made my day by giving me copies of more photographs and a wonderful pot of homemade raspberry jam. The family were escorted next door, right upstairs to the servants' quarters and into the garden – sadly, no longer the tended lawns and rosebeds of yesteryear. The section of the original garden, where the tennis court was, is now four detached houses, designed by architects, Carter and Chu, in 1982.

The family were able to sense very clearly where their ancestors had grown up, but for Wilfred's daughter, perhaps there was a sense of closure from this visit. Wilfred had died in 1943, when his daughter was only eight years old. It was wartime and she was away at boarding school. She recalls being woken and told of her father's death, but there was no hope of getting home to be with her mother due to travel restrictions. It can't have been easy, facing a past she had so little direct contact with, but one which she so dearly wanted; I believe she was fascinated to see the old family home.

The Wood family were very wealthy. Peter Frederick Wood's (let's call him, as I discovered the family do, 'Peter Fred') grandfather was a very successful Manchester businessman, and the family wealth just seemed to accumulate from then on.

Peter Fred is an occupational enigma: it remains a mystery as to precisely what he did for a living. His family understand him to have been in a partnership in a mill in Yorkshire, but that's such a vague reference that it tells us almost nothing. Born in 1848, he is listed in the 1881 census as a 'retired worsted spinner', retired at the age of 33! He certainly was fortunate. At that time, Peter Fred and Emily were living in North Meols, Lancashire. By 1891, he was here in Lubbock Road and 'living on his own means'. No occupation is listed in 1901 or 1911.

Becky told me that Peter Fred had begun a family chronology, which stated that 'some' of the children – possibly only the boys – were at Miss Milkinson's School in Chislehurst, and their governess – for the girls, perhaps – was a Miss Caldwell. In 1911, the household is one of 15 rooms, with a cook, parlour maid, housemaid and between maid.

Peter Fred invested his fortune, inherited from his father, in the shares of the Great Western Railway; the income from these presumably funded his lifestyle. But what did he do all day? I knew the family were staunch Methodists and, as such, there would not have been much wining and dining. In 1891, he was visiting family in North Meols, and I have learned that the family got together regularly for Christmas and holidays. Peter Fred was elected a member of the Royal Geographic Society in April 1893;

he was also a member of the National Club at Whitehall Gardens SW1.

The more likely explanation is given in the memorial book written about Emily. Emily was from a family of cotton spinners, a highly regarded family in Southport, and benefactors of Mornington Road Methodist Chapel in the town. The memorial sketch is a wonderful piece of high Victorian hyperbole, written with the weight of sorrowing grief. In 1886, chiefly on account of Mrs Wood's health, which had never been strong, the family moved to Chislehurst, and for some time she seemed to improve and to gain strength from the change of air. Chislehurst was never a spa town, but it was reputed to be a healthy place to live. Most likely, in reality, because persons of fortune and distinction seemed to prosper here, more in terms of their wealth than health! I subsequently found other Wood relatives living at the Manor House on Manor Park Road, so Peter Fred may well have had a recommendation to come south.

The sketch continues: 'Mrs Wood was a most devoted and self sacrificing mother, but she never forgot her children's higher nature while looking after their bodily health. She ever strove to draw their young hearts to the saviour, and to implant in them Bible truths by giving them scripture lessons and by gathering them around her on Sunday evenings, reading and talking to them. She devoted herself increasingly to her family, especially in time of illness, and probably, on several occasions considerably injured herself thereby'.

This is the only mention in the little book about her children, of whom there were five in total: Margaret, Peter Norris, Wilfred Burton, Editha and Frederick Gordon. True to Victorian values of morality and Christian calling, it seems that Emily had other boys to minister to. 'The deep interest which Mrs Wood took in work amongst boys' is recounted in the memorial sketch.

She once said it was her only work and she must give her best to it. Through contact with the Children's Special Service Mission at LLanfairfechan in North Wales (later to become the Scripture Union), she began to feel that God had work for her amongst 'those most difficult beings'. The little telegraph messengers had attracted her attention. Hearing that there was a special organisation for their benefit, known as the Telegraph Messengers' Christian Association, she at once resolved to open a branch at Chislehurst immediately on her return. There were about a dozen boys in Mrs Wood's Bible class, which met from time to time in one of the rooms at Camden Lodge, which had a little organ chamber attached. Here, they used to sing

Peter Frederick Wood

Emily Wood

Frederick Gordon Wood, 1914
Royal Naval Reserve

Camden Lodge 1886

Entrance to the organ chamber

Editha and Margaret (Marnie) Wood

Farringtons School Chapel Window

hymns and she would accompany them on the organ, for she knew how to play skilfully. 'How greatly she rejoiced if she saw the good seed springing and growing up in the souls of any one of them'.

Emily herself wrote, 'We had a nice time together, we sang some hymns and then had a little talk by the fire, and they were so attentive and interested. I feel I must do something; they are growing up so quickly. I am fond of them, and I ought to be, they are so nice to me'. The last time the telegraph messengers' class assembled at Camden Lodge was on 8 January 1904, when Mr Geoffrey Pocklington from Sherborne came to give a special address. Mrs Wood was suffering but tried hard to bear up. However, she had to be carried up to bed before the boys came. She was loved and respected by the Chislehurst Post Office boys, and the deep feeling with which they regarded her was shown by a letter they sent testifying to the genuineness of their appreciation.

Her vocabulary is a matter of amusement to me now, but she obviously felt very strongly about the spiritual guidance given to 'her boys'. Today's generation would see the following passage very differently. In 1902, she wrote, 'I have had the most glorious word to-day from Ipswich. At the Bible Class yesterday afternoon several of the boys "came out"! I have felt almost empowered to-day by the love and goodness of this distinct answer to prayer, this is more than good, it is wonderful.'

She enjoyed the light, bracing mountain air of Llanfairfechan. She wrote from there, on 31 May 1904, that 'life is a battle, and sometimes one's heart gets overwhelmed, but we must keep our eyes fixed on our Captain, I can do all things through Christ'. She had always hoped the invigorating air would benefit her, but here, in spite of the skill and care of the doctors and nurses, the insidious disease made its fatal progress. A few weeks before the end, she rallied, but the great wave of heat in July proved too much for her enfeebled condition. There was a considerable congregation of relatives and friends at Mornington Road for the funeral service. She was laid to rest in the Southport cemetery of her family.

That might have been my only insight into this distinctive family but for the musings of another writer in the wider family. Lucy M. Boston, author of the Greene Knowe books for children, was Peter Fred's niece, and I am grateful to her for some insights into Peter Fred's character in her autobiography, *Perverse and Foolish*.

Peter Fred used to bring his family to Southport for Christmas. Lucy Boston describes him as a man of 'passionate neuroses'. Emily was apparently tall, elegant and very kind, but after her death, all of Peter Fred's crankiness rioted, unchecked. At last, I was getting the true picture of this idiosyncratic man. Lucy continues, 'His family all spoke of him with frustration and despair, Peter Fred was a blight on all their lives! One daughter had been turned out and cut off absolutely for becoming a Roman Catholic. The eldest daughter who kept house for him had become a physical wreck, but she had such an explosive fund of feeling that she never stopped talking and could not speak at less than the highest pressure. She thus made a perpetual joke of herself, but never resented laughter'.

Uncle Peter Fred, recalls Lucy – whatever his domestic faults – had warm, formal manners in family gatherings, and he did not forget his nephews' and nieces' names. After lunch, they would go in to the library for prayers, taken by him. Peter Fred had a 'thrilling personal voice' and read superbly, looking down at the Scriptures through pince-nez set crookedly on his nose, and his chin thrust out in affirmation.

Peter Norris's story cannot fail to move you. The eldest son, he was, however, educated at home due to his asthma, but spent two years in School House at the Leys School, Cambridge, from the age of 17. He worked as an insurance clerk for a firm of underwriters at Lloyd's of London. He was a Sunday school teacher at the Methodist Church, and it is likely that this is where he met his future wife, Kathleen Mawe.

Yvonne contacted me subsequently, to tell me that William Mawe lived at Hatton House in Lubbock Road with his wife Hannah: these were the parents of Frederick Mawe, whose daughter was Kathleen. The Mawe family were originally from Worcestershire and had made a fortune from the drapery business. Kathleen's brothers are also listed on the 'served and survived' memorial in the Methodist Church, which is why I assume Peter and Kathleen not only had the road in common but also active church worship.

Yvonne's detailed research from the local newspapers provides the painful detail of Peter's death. At the outbreak of war, the call came for volunteers, and Peter joined as a private in the 4th Royal Field Ambulance Royal Field Reserve. His asthma most likely barred him from active service. In March 1915, he was promoted to lance corporal and eventually posted to the King's Own Royal Regiment (Lancaster), reflecting his Southport roots. In 1916, he was sent to Amara in Mesopotamia, (Iraq) where he served with great distinction. The Mesopotamian Expeditionary Force had been in Amara since June 1915, and it immediately became a hospital centre. The accommodation for medical units on both banks of the river was greatly increased during 1916; seven general hospitals and some smaller units were stationed there. At the time of his death, Peter Norris had reached the rank of second lieutenant. His brother, Wilfred, now a doctor, was also stationed at Amara, and was present at his death. He 'died of his wounds' is the common phrase, but the truth is more brutal. I understand from his family that both his legs were shot off and he died in Wilfred's arms on 19 January 1917. He was 36 years old. He is buried at the Amara War Cemetery, on the left bank of the Tigris. Peter is remembered on the roll of honour in the Chislehurst Methodist Church 'Called, and Chosen and Faithful', and his name is inscribed on his mother's grave in Southport. The words chiselled in stone are: 'These for faith and loyalty shrank not from the bitter fight'.

Peter and Kathleen had married in late 1915; she was a widow less than eighteen months later. They had little chance to conceive children, and she never remarried. She died in 1972 at the age of 85. She was living in Malvern, as was her brother; perhaps she moved to be near her family when they left Chislehurst after 1911. During our afternoon tea, reference was made to 'Auntie Norris', who always sent 'ten bob' to Wilfred's children at Christmas.

The aforementioned Wilfred Burton survived the war, married a cousin and had a career of some distinction. He also attended the Leys with his brother and went on to Jesus College, Cambridge. He first worked as a house surgeon at the Victoria Hospital, Chelsea, and then went to St Bartholomew's. On returning to England after the war, he started his public health career in the Tilbury Dock area as a tuberculosis officer. He spent most of his spare time and weekends at the London Chest Hospital and, whilst studying, was put on the honorary staff of that hospital. Renowned for his profound knowledge of radiographic images of the lungs, he was elected a fellow of the Royal College of Physicians in 1940. 'His command of the English language was extraordinary; he had the gift of expressing thoughts in a telling, interesting and often humorous manner. He was never afraid to express his opinions often in a forthright manner; he was a most delightful colleague'. He does not seem to have been too much of a chip off the old block!

Frederick Gordon, the second Wood child to be born in Lubbock Road, may have been the child most like both his parents combined. He went to boarding school in Southport with his cousin James Heald Wood. Frederick Gordon took an MA in Natural Sciences from Cambridge; he was also a

Fellow of the Royal Geographic Society, like his father. Family ties were very strong. Caldicott School, where Gordon became head teacher for a while, had been founded by his cousin James in 1904. James's wife was Theodora Caldicott Ingram, hence, in all likelihood, the name of the school. In 1911, Frederick Gordon was visiting friends in Llanfairfechan and is listed as a schoolmaster part-time and a student part-time. In 1912, the Scouts group began at the school. Gordon was a very keen Scoutmaster, and it became a strong interest at the school.

Like his brothers, Frederick Gordon joined up. He was a leading telegraphist with the Royal Naval Reserve in 1914, a wireless officer – Morse code and all that. His First World War certificate lists him as having a scar on his temple: I wonder if this was from a brotherly skirmish, or perhaps he fell against the organ! In 1928, again following family interest, he was elected a fellow of the Royal Astronomical Society. In 1932, there was a dedication service for the opening of the school chapel with an organ. Gordon was the organist – must have got that from his mother! In 1936, Gordon became joint headmaster at the school.

Frederick Gordon died in May 1944, in Farnham Royal Hospital, of congestive heart failure. He was listed as a schoolmaster at Caldicott School, but no longer as head teacher. Wilfred's wife, another Lucy – only recently widowed – was with him when he died, but his sisters were not present.

Margaret Heald Wood, the eldest child, was known as 'Marnie' and clearly had a spinster daughter's life at the beck and call of her difficult father. She is, however, remembered in stained glass in the chapel of Farringtons School, so I'm glad to know she had some outside life. She moved to an hotel in Woking, dying in Kettlewell Nursing Home in 1955. She left an estate worth £37,000, and is buried at Wilfred's home in Essex.

Editha Agnes, the younger daughter – but the first child to be born at Camden Lodge – had a very different life and, I hope, a happier one. Described as 'eccentric' by her descendants, apparently, she obtained a motor bike, and family folklore has it that – turning up on it late one evening – she was barred from the house. Indeed, she was never to return. Editha converted to Catholicism, trained as an art student and teacher, and lived in Kensington, London. Her father was said to be 'horrified'. She was the last direct survivor of the family, dying at Cromwell Avenue, Highgate, in 1958, leaving only £1,000.

Peter Fred died in Aston Grey's Nursing Home in Bournemouth, but his death certificate still lists Camden Lodge as his residence. He died of a cerebral thrombosis brought on by a serious kidney disorder and hardening of the arteries. It's very interesting that both he and his wife had significant kidney conditions; others in Lubbock Road died of nephritis – Frederick Freese for one – and I'm not placing any blame, but perhaps the Victorian plumbing system was below par! Peter Fred's death was reported by the local doctor, with no family in attendance. No matter how lacking in filial goodwill they may have been, Peter Fred left three of his children £100,000 to share. He is buried alongside his wife in Southport; he was 92. The inscription on his grave is: 'Blessed are they that feel his testimonies'. I somehow doubt that Editha felt that blessed; I wonder if she even attended the service?

Camden Lodge may not have been the happiest family home, but it is still standing. It probably owes its survival to Peter Fred's longevity and wealth. It was split into flats after 1930 and occupied by some distinctive characters. One late resident, born in Egypt and married to the editor of *Horse and Hound* magazine, was described as 'impossibly chic' by her godson.

Camden Lodge (right) and The Rookery, aerial view, 1937

12. The Rookery

1887 - 1908
Alfred Constans Mitchell: A Single Man and his Steel Pens

Being my own home, until 2015, this is where my research truly began. I had a number of original deeds left to me by our vendors and I was transfixed by the life of a man with a curious name who seemingly lived alone in this large house with plenty of garden.

Alfred Constans Mitchell was the first owner of The Rookery, which is now known as 'Brackens', 68 Lubbock Road. He is typical of the entrepreneurial class of businessmen who made Chislehurst their home following the arrival of the railway and the opening up of the Camden Park Estate as a prime residential location.

He was the senior of the two London partners of the firm William Mitchell, Steel Pen and Penholder Makers, Birmingham. He was born in 1839, the second son of the founder of the eponymous firm. Educated privately, he was raised to take part in the family business from a young age. William Mitchell enjoyed a world-wide reputation and was one of the first workers in the pen trade. The London House was established in 1855 in Falcon Square, subsequently moving to 44 Cannon Street. At the time, it

The Rookery, now Brackens, 68 Lubbock Road

was one of the most well-known business houses in London.

In 1843, Mitchell's had started the manufacture of what became their celebrated 'Letter' pens: these were distinguished by their bright, prominently-embossed letters of the alphabet, each letter representing a pen distinct in shape and action, and made to suit some calligraphic requirement. It was for this 'letter' series that the business was specially noted. The 'J' pen was the best known and most successful example. It was with one of the 'N' pens that the King of Denmark, Christian IX, signed the New Convention in 1863; this pen could be seen under a glass case at Rosenberg Schloss, Copenhagen, for many years. The firm also supplied pens for the special use of the Prince of Wales (before he became Edward VII) and other members of the royal family, and were also pen makers to the Government and the Bank of England. The firm adopted the arms of the City of London for their trade mark.

The firm expanded rapidly, benefiting from mechanical scientific advances in Birmingham to perfect the manufacture of their pens. Over 1,000,000 pens were produced yearly and, since opening, Mitchell's maintained a reputation for the improvements it introduced in the quality of production. Wherever the firm exhibited, after 1851, they gained the highest awards, including many gold medals both at home and abroad. The illustration of their exhibition pyramid – which went to the 1889 Paris Exhibition – is a work of art in itself!

When I contacted the Pen Room Museum in Birmingham, it was thought that Alfred was a dormant partner in the business. However, a search in *The Leading Men of London* has a specific sketch of him. There is no record of him attending the regular board meetings in Birmingham, since it is clear that he was running the London end of the business. The business was run initially by William's widow, Sarah, and then, increasingly, by her four sons, following William's death in 1845. Aurelius Bruce, the eldest son, and Francis William Victor, the youngest, ran the Birmingham operation, becoming partners in 1863; meanwhile, Alfred Constans, and his younger brother, Theodore Albert, managed the London branch.

In 1871, Alfred and Theodore were living together off Logs Hill, listing their occupation as 'merchants'. By 1881, Alfred is lodging in Church Row, Chislehurst, and references to him in Lubbock Road appear in Kelly's Directory from 1889. Theodore lived at Elmstead Glade, in Walden Road, with his large family. He is listed as a trustee of Christ Church, and is a signatory to the land purchase from Nathaniel Strode in 1872. So the

The Mitchell family, including William, top centre, and his sons on the bottom row, left to right: Alfred, Theodore, Aurelius and Francis

44, Cannon Street, the business headquarters

1889 Paris Exhibition Pyramid display

brothers were obviously settled in the area, commuting daily to Cannon Street by train. I suspect Alfred commissioned the building of what became known as The Rookery. There is a farm on the site of Rookery Road Board School, Handsworth, near where Alfred and his brothers grew up; it's just possible, though obviously inconclusive, that this is where he took the name from. The Rookery was a substantial Victorian home of 15 rooms, according to the 1911 census, and I can only conclude that Alfred anticipated marrying and having a large family, just like his brother. However, the 1891 census shows him living at The Rookery alone with a butler, housekeeper – who doubled as the cook – and a house maid. It's the same picture in 1901: his niece from Birmingham is staying with him, but there are still more staff in the house than those they are working for. The house stood in two acres of land, so I am surprised not to see a gardener listed as well!

Alfred, like so many of his contemporaries, was a member of Gresham's and of other clubs. The business was thriving – indeed, it still exists today, under the amalgamated business name of British Pens – but by the turn of the century, Alfred's health was in decline. He died at the end of February 1908, nursed by his mother at the family home, Augustus Road, Edgbaston. The immediate cause of death was pneumonia, but he had been suffering from endocarditis for the previous eighteen months. This is an inflammation of the inside lining of the heart chambers and heart valves; he may have had an abnormality of the heart all his life. Today, with modern medicine, he would have been treated with antibiotics and even surgery, but at the turn of the last century, his life chances were always going to be limited. He left an estate worth £44,644, and The Rookery was sold by the trustees of his estate: his brothers, Aurelius, Theodore and Francis.

1908 - 1937
The Harwood Family: In Search of Hilda

The Harwood's story has much resonance for me; it was beguiling to unravel. Horace Harwood was a solicitor in London. Hilda was his wife. Prior to coming to Chislehurst, the family had lived in a Nineteenth Century villa in Longlands Road, Sidcup. I had come to this particular house from a Victorian semi in Sidcup and the legal profession sustained my family! Horace worked for Stephenson Harwood, a law firm which still exists. It was easy to make contact and fortuitously they had a booklet on the history of the firm, written for a centenary in 1978. I am the sort of person who now waits in happy trepidation for the footstep of the postman (the postman had trepidations for another reason as my dog wasn't the most welcoming in the road). I delight in receiving death certificates and wills and on this occasion, it was a seemingly arid blue booklet that got my heart pounding.

The firm of Stephenson Harwood & Co. was founded by William Harwood, older brother to Horace. Horace retired in 1927 at the age of 69. I suppose I was a little disappointed that the booklet did not contain any photographs but the archives of the firm had been destroyed in a fire. The paper trail was plentiful enough. There are many examples of the travels that Horace undertook over the years from 1921 to 1929. His journeys took him from Durban to London in 1921, Shanghai to Southampton via Madeira in 1922, Bombay in 1925 and 1926 and Australia in 1929. He travelled alone, as far as I can see. Horace lived for a further 10 years at The Rookery, dying on 18 March 1937 leaving an estate worth £66,463 before the sale of the property. He is buried in St Nicholas churchyard.

Having learned a little about Horace, my next quest was naturally his wife and children. Horace was married to Hilda Branson, the daughter of a high court judge in India. The 1891 census gave me her age and place of birth. Hilda was a child of the Empire, born in Bycullah, Bombay in August 1872. (Her father was Reginald Montague Auber Branson; a pupil of Rugby School, graduate of Jesus College, Cambridge and a barrister from Middle Temple. He was an Advocate at the Madras High Court of Judicature becoming Advocate General of Bombay).

That was too exciting to let go, Ancestry became my best friend and I spent many happy hours messing about looking at other people's family trees. Hilda was the middle one of five children. Theirs was a fascinating family with a reasonably good trail to follow. My first dabble into the family gleaned the facts that Hilda's older sister and eldest child was an actress and divorced. Her older brother, Vivian, was a Major in the Indian army and died childless aged 40. Her younger brother, Ernest, became a coffee and rubber plantation owner with a daughter (girls are frustrating for genealogists as the trail can go cold if they marry and change names) and finally her youngest brother, three years her junior, Lionel Hugh, an army officer, married with male offspring.

Lionel turned out to be quite a find! Google and the 1891 census combined to provide a hilarious turn of events and a glorious discovery about Hilda. Lionel was in the army but seemingly spent a lot of his 'spare' time learning conjuring tricks! When I saw an entry in Google that he was the author of *Indian Conjuring Tricks*, I had to find the book. It was a bit of a let-down, being a 'print on demand' copy the illustrations were not forthcoming. I do, though, now know how to approach the Indian Rope Trick, so may be my money was well spent after all! However, there was a list of other publications by the same author and here was my salvation. *A Lifetime of Deception* by L H Branson, an autobiography. Bingo! Might this tell me about his sister?

The book arrived, a discontinued book from Castleford Public Library, smelling beautifully musty with softened old pages. It didn't fit in my dog-proof letter box and was sitting tantalisingly on my door step when I got home one afternoon. Another day when I've got some time I will read it from cover to cover but on this occasion, I skimmed fast for references to Hilda, Horace or Chislehurst.

Lionel mentioned early on that at the age of ten he was a boarder at Bedford Grammar School; a Google check assured me that the school still exists. Public Schools are fantastic when it comes to alumni records, naturally I sent an e mail immediately to the Old Boys Club!

The book had deceived me, in that there was so little information about Lionel's childhood where I imagined I might have learned more about Hilda. There was one mention of Chislehurst, in that there seems to have been a desperate search for a nanny to look after Lionel's two young boys in Chislehurst in 1909 and a subsequent reference to their living in Bickley. At the beginning of 1914 they were permanently in England. His mother, he says, had squandered a fortune and needed a small allowance to help her live in comfort in London. But he did confirm that his sons were also pupils at Bedford so that gave me cause for hope that the school would have another generation's information, taking me ever closer to living relatives!

An e mail from Bedford school popped into my in box which I shall always treasure. Lionel Hugh Branson (known as Hugh) was indeed a pupil at Bedford. He entered the school in May 1890 leaving at the end of the Autumn term 1895. His address was given as High Court, Bombay. A mention is given of a guardian, Mr H G Harwood of London. Now that was promising, Hilda's husband, Horace. The e mail continues It would appear that Hugh had two sons who came to the school, Clive at the school 1921 – 1925, he is listed as going into the Hong Kong and Shanghai bank – I wonder if Uncle Horace had a hand in that appointment? Anthony Hugh Chimmo Branson entered May 1922 and left in 1927, he became an architect. Their parents first address was – wait for it – The Rookery, Lubbock Road, Chislehurst and their guardian was given as their aunt..... Mrs Hilda Harwood.

I was overjoyed at this point. Firstly, that the connection had been confirmed but secondly that occupation of architect meant I could possibly get an address from a professional register. Could Anthony still be alive?

I discovered the Branson family had pedigree and found a recent entry in Debretts relating to descendants of 'Tony'. He had died in 1989. This is where my stalking period really began. With some trepidation I put a letter into the post to Nigel Branson, son of Tony, great nephew of Hilda! I included my telephone contact in the letter.

I tend not to answer calls from numbers I don't recognise but absent mindedly I took this particular call. Hallelujah, an educated voice was saying 'Branson here,' (for two tiny seconds I wondered why the railway magnate of Virgin fame was calling me until I came to my senses). Nigel Branson was utterly charming but very matter of fact; he didn't really know the name Harwood but thought his sister would be the best person to speak to as she held all the family information. He did add the glorious quote that he knew his father had been somewhat in awe of his 'domineering aunts' and remembered stifling meals in a panelled dining room where he was not allowed to talk and certainly not leave the table until every mouthful was consumed. Wow, the dining room of 68 was panelled, it had to be the same place.

It's always the women of the family that hold the key to family trees isn't it? Nigel's sister, Denise, lived in Canada, she was able to confirm that the aged aunts, Ada and Hilda, were not really that old, mid to late forties, but to a lonely little boy dinner may have been a horrible experience. Denise recounted a story regaled by her father - One day they had roast beef and Tony didn't like all the fat so he left it on the side of his plate. When the butler came to take his plate, he was told to leave it as "Master Branson was saving that 'til last, as that was his favourite", he was left alone to eat the fat until it was finished. The next evening, he was given a plate of cold fat to eat as "that was his favourite". How cruel. I used to think fondly of Hilda but I'm going to reserve judgement now and hope it was Ada playing the part of the bully.

So I was forming a picture of the former residents of my own home, one that is not complete without knowledge of the children. Horace and Hilda had two children, born in Sidcup, Gerald, 24 July 1894, and Evelyn in 1898.

Initially Gerald attended Marlborough House School in Sidcup then progressed to Amesbury School in Bickley. He went to Marlborough College in May 1908. His end of term grade hovers around the middle to lower quartile of the class. It seems that he did not find academic work much to his taste. There are early absences which may have been due to illness or to receiving private tuition at home. He joined the Officers Training Corps whilst at school. The school also recorded his height and weight which was 64.5 inches and 123 lbs aged 13 and 10 months in 1908 and 68.7 inches and 160 lbs in the summer of 1911 when he left, aged 16 and 10 months.

At the outbreak of war, he was serving his articles with his father to become a solicitor but he at once applied for a commission in an infantry regiment. As his appointment did not come as soon as he had hoped, he enlisted in the Honourable Artillery Corps, and went out to the Front with the first contingent of that regiment. After a few months, he was invalided home suffering from acute rheumatism. One wonders if this was why he was studying at home in his earlier academic life. After a short time at home he was gazetted as a subaltern in the 3rd Suffolk's and after the usual training was back at the Front. He was invalided home twice more with rheumatism and suffering from gas poisoning and shell shock.

In February 1916, he was seconded for service to India. Shortly after his arrival he was detailed for special duty in connection with the Viceroy's visit and received from His Excellency a memento of the occasion. Given Gerald's family ties with the sub continent it was not a surprising secondment. After about a year in India he was sent to Egypt to qualify as a pilot with the Royal Flying Corps. From there he was sent to Salonica where he performed excellent service on that Front before finally meeting with an accident and was sent home. After a rest, he returned to light duties at Tadcaster, acting as an instructor. He was then appointed to ferry pilot and stayed with the Central Despatch Pool for many months.

Being keen to serve in India again, he applied for duty there and was appointed to the 97th Squadron which was stationed at Ford Junction, West Sussex. He met with his death the day after reporting at Ford and just three hours before he was due to sail for India. To have come all through the devastation of war, his end is all the more tragic for its futility.

Gerald's fate was known to me as one of six Lubbock Road boys to be named on the Chislehurst War Memorial. My father had recently given me a copy of *For King and Country*. I was reading it in bed one evening, when I noticed the name 'The Rookery', my very own house. I was probably reading this tragic story in this very boy's bedroom or maybe that of his poor parents. The description of his death in the local newspaper, kindly forwarded to me by Yvonne, is detailed and sad.

Gerald died aged 24, 1 May 1919, as the result of an accident while flying at the Ford Aerodrome. Yvonne told me that his was still considered a war death as he was in uniform. Gerald had taken one of the latest types of machine from London and was making a short flight from the aerodrome with two others on board. The machine had nearly completed a semi-circle of the aerodrome, when it suddenly went into a left-hand spin, and crashed to earth from a height of nearly 100 feet. The coroner recorded a verdict of 'accidentally killed whilst flying'. Only one passenger survived sustaining a broken arm.

The final piece of information makes me weep: he was to have been married shortly after his arrival in India, this surely added pathos to his untimely death.

He was buried in St Nicholas churchyard (where his father would also be buried, two decades later) under an attractive white marble cross. I learned from the logbooks of St Nicholas Primary School that all the boys attended his military funeral. His parents, Evelyn and his Branson Grandmother attended the funeral along with Aunt Ada and her husband, Hugh's wife, Winnie Chimmo Branson and his sister's future in laws. Floral tributes were received from Uncle William, who was also his Godfather, and his Grandmother, Mrs Ethel Harwood, the staff of Stephenson Harwood "The Duds", from Lubbock Road neighbours, the Straus family of Hatton Cottage and Mr and Mrs Fehr of Hatton House but most poignantly of all from a Miss Maynie Thomason in Bombay, his intended?

The family could have descended into deep despair but were soon able to look forward to a wedding. Evelyn married Louis Allard Stonard almost a year later at Christ Church in Lubbock Road on 28 April 1920. I wonder if the bride walked the 500 yards to the church with her father? Louis was 26 and lived at Albemarle Grange, Mavelstone Road, a stone's throw from The Rookery. His war record has him decorated with a star in 1915 with the Artillery Corps; it's just possible that he was a friend of Gerald's, they were the same age. He was listed as a merchant at the time of his marriage; his parents had an upholstery and grocery businesses in London. Evelyn was 22.

The story could end there but I was left at this juncture with two loose ends. Did the Harwoods have any grandchildren and what happened to Hilda? Luckily Ancestry had some further clues. Passenger lists give some wonderful information, home address, overseas address, occupation and port of final destination. I found Louis Allard and Evelyn Stonard incoming from Durban in 1927, possibly to celebrate her father's retirement. They were both travelling again from Mombasa in 1938, bear in mind that Horace died in 1937, were they coming to the UK to see to matters following her father's death? Their intended final residence was listed as 'other part of the British Empire' and Allard was listed as a farmer in South Rhodesia.

I suddenly found myself embroiled in the history of the Empire, Cecil Rhodes et al. I never found a death certificate for Louis or Allard as I was to learn he called himself as the Zimbabwe record office was not open to public view; surprise, surprise. About to give up, I had an amazingly lucky break. We were on holiday after Christmas in New York when a new email popped up in my in box. I had at least a month earlier made contact with the South African National Archives and lo and behold a late Christmas gift came my way: the death certificate and will of Evelyn Stonard. No one speak to me, this was a 15 page document of intense interest and as it turned out, intrigue!

Evelyn made her will in 1965 as a widow; so at least I knew Allard was dead by 1965. The will was available outside Rhodesia, my contact in South Africa told me, because Evelyn had property in Pretoria. Evelyn died on 24 May 1971 at 1 Lowood Flats, Borrowdale, Salisbury, Rhodesia. She was cremated at Warren Hills, aged 73. She had had cancer of the stomach for 9 months. The death certificate gave the name of the undertakers and at this point I probably did go mad but I even contacted them to see if they had a record of her husband's death. They were most polite in response but couldn't help!

I was still left with the question of where was Hilda? My Facebook status received a lot of 'likes' when I felt I was closing in on her. It was the passenger lists that provided the best clues. I knew that The Rookery was sold in 1937 following Horace's death; If Evelyn was permanently abroad there would be no sense in hanging on to such a sizable property. Hilda may never have travelled when Horace was alive but she made significant journeys as his widow. On 6 April 1939 she is listed as travelling to South Africa, leaving her English residence, Coombe Lea presumably to visit her daughter. I am told Coombe Lea, (now a cul de sac bearing the same name), was the sort of establishment where ladies like Hilda's made their home. A second entry has her returning to Coombe Lea, on 9 September 1939, auspicious timing with the outbreak of the Second World War.

The final known movement I have found for Hilda is 22 February 1946, departing the UK, from Wood Hays, Willow Grove (now flats) for Cape Town. The war was over; she needed to see her daughter and she was herself now 73. I have no record of her death or burial, her wider family has no record of her passing. I assume she died in Rhodesia, staying with Evelyn, in the late 1940's or early 50's. She remains my final piece of the jigsaw, my conundrum, my ghost!

Evelyn's will is another story in itself. She obviously had been a successful businesswoman in the field of tobacco farming, and add to that the sole beneficiary of the Harwood estate on the death of her mother. The will is detailed and caused trouble as I discovered from more stalking.

Four faithful servants, Joswa, Ndireya, Lembani and Maluza each received £50. Her god daughter, Linda Verwoerd, received £500 (so I don't think there were any Harwood grandchildren) and her late husbands' god son received £500. Former employees David Tomlinson and Conway Broadbent received £10,000 and £2,000 respectively and then there were bequests to charities: £10,000 each to Red Cross Society of Rhodesia and the Rhodesian Society for the Prevention of Tuberculosis – was that the cause of Allard's death? £5,000 to Rhodesian Society for the Prevention of Cruelty to Animals, ah she was a cat lover. And then the biggee; the remainder of her estate and effects to be invested to assist in setting up a Law Student Society of Rhodesia and a bursary fund for students showing aptitude and desire for a degree in Law, to be known as the Harwood Trust. Evelyn was fully aware of the political situation; the will clearly states that 'in the event of sanctions still being in operation by the United Kingdom Government then the legacies should be paid out of my South African estate until such time as my English estate is released from embargo'.

Then there was a codicil, I nearly had apoplexy. Bequests were being made to nephews and nieces in the UK, Stonard relations with addresses. I was back to the potential of living relatives. A quick perusal of census information for Allard's family revealed a brother and two sisters, all of whom had married and had issue. The recipients were to get money and jewellery, a diamond and emerald ring and a gold and pearl star brooch. One of the addresses was in Chislehurst. Being very brave I went for a drive, the address looked like the sort of house where an established family lived so I dropped a note through the door explaining as best I could that I trying to complete an historic jigsaw puzzle.

The next morning, I answered my phone to a number I didn't know but recognised as local; the good old Imperial Chislehurst 467 code. It was the wife of Allard's nephew and she would be happy to come around for coffee. Sensibly, she had checked with a mutual friend/neighbour that I wasn't totally mad and it was safe to take coffee from me! 'Ursula' knew some of the story but couldn't throw any light on Hilda's death. The Harwood Trust does not exist, the family had serious difficulty getting any information regarding the will and the funds were seemingly embezzled by one of the trustees. The jewellery did make its way to the beneficiaries however and Ursula still has the brooch, but as a symbol of lack of inheritance it is not a beloved item.

The story does not really have a happy ending, or maybe it does. Over coffee we agreed that Evelyn's intentions had always been for the very best, she had no idea what would actually happen after her death. Maybe now the brooch will get a new lease of life. As she was leaving Ursula said, "You did know she was called Tubby, didn't you"? Poor Evelyn, did her big brother tease her, was she overweight? Again, we shall never know, but to Tubby, Gerald, Horace and especially Hilda, wherever you are, I am immensely grateful for this journey of delightful discovery. We can only live in hope as the inscription on Gerald's grave (pictured below) says "Beyond the river of death – love lives – as yesterday – so forever".

Gerald Harwood's grave in the churchyard of St Nicholas Chislehurst

Potentially, but not conclusively, Hillside, Lubbock Road, 1881

13. Abbey Lodge and Hillside

1876 - 1901
Colonel Hugh Adams Silver: Rubber Balls in Silvertown

Just as in the game of Cleudo, we have a mystery with Abbey Lodge, with leading character Colonel Silver. Luckily, there is no murder victim (though if we were to believe the story starring David Suchet, filmed at Abbey Lodge, this was the setting for ghastly murders in the basement!)

You'd think that with such a substantial house there would be evidence of the architect and its first occupants, but it is all less than clear. The first time Abbey Lodge appears on a census is in 1891, occupied by Colonel Hugh Adams Silver. A man of distinction: on deeper investigation, it appears that Silvertown in the London Docklands is named after him. Abbey Lodge was not his first home in Lubbock Road and this is the start of the mystery. Hugh spent his early married life in Hampstead. In 1876, he arrived in Lubbock Road to live at 'Hillside'.

Tracing the information on Hillside has been inconclusive and frustrating. The plot on which the house stood was next door to that of John Lubbock, as identified on the 1862 map. From early indentures, I knew the first occupant was William R. Winch, a tea merchant and founding trustee of Christ Church, but I couldn't get enough leads on his story. There is an 1881 drawing of a particularly substantial house called Hillside in Chislehurst, by architect Joseph D. Moye: this house is built on a slope above the road, all of which tallies with the Camden Park landscape, but I cannot conclusively tie it to Lubbock Road..

Colonel Silver came to Hillside with 11 children. The Colonel's eldest daughter, Elizabeth, had married from the family home in Hampstead in February 1875, but by October the following year, her mother, Annie Ellen Silver, was dead (the death certificate records her residence as Hillside, Chislehurst). I don't think the stress of the move out of London killed her, but it's entirely possible that the family moved in order to gain a quieter life for the sake of her health.

Annie was only 46 when she passed away. The immediate cause of death was apoplexy but she was probably a long-term sufferer of epilepsy; she'd had three days of convulsions. Eleven children and epilepsy: that's a tough card to have drawn. Clearly, there was not yet any great affiliation with Chislehurst; Annie was buried back at St John's, Hampstead, although

Reverend Fleming officiated at the service. From this point on, this story is easier to follow, as the evidence is abundant.

The Colonel's second son, Stephen Winkworth – named after his paternal grandfather – married in 1878, and is listed as resident in Chislehurst. Hugh re-married in 1879. His bride was Anne Cornish, 27 years his junior, and three more children were born at Hillside before 1881. But then comes the switch. I came across a reference – on eBay, of all places – to an 1884 indenture for land forming part of the Camden Park Estate between – guess who? – yep, Nathaniel William John Strode and Lt. Col. Hugh Adams Silver. It could have revealed so much information – it was four pages long! – but, sadly, the sale was unidentified and the information lost, to me at least. Though in fact it probably just outlines all the conditions of Nat's building requirements, which I have seen in many other detailed indentures of that time.

With eight children still at home, something even bigger than Hillside may have been required. Maybe Anne wanted her own home, not that of her husband's first wife. We will never know, but it does seem that the family moved directly across the road to the newly-built five-storey house that they called Abbey Lodge (now Chislehurst Hall). Hillside was then occupied

The site of the demolished Hillside, with Lamas next door

by Reverend Fleming, whilst the long search for a permanent parsonage began. When Fleming died in 1900, Col. and Mrs Silver attended his funeral. The 1937 aerial photograph of the road shows the substantial plot next to Lamas where Hillside had been recently demolished. The name lives on as the name of the current house at number 99.

The Colonel was a multi-millionaire, inheriting the family business (the manufacture and distribution of waterproof rubber clothing), with a factory in Greenwich. S.W. Silver & Co began in Cornhill in 1798 as colonial and army agents, clothiers and outfitters principally to those in the army and Colonial Service, as well as acting as shipping agents for such people travelling overseas. Hence Hugh describing himself as an 'Australian merchant' in the 1871 census. In 1852, the business moved to an undeveloped site in Woolwich Reach on the north bank of the Thames. A town grew up around the factory which became known as Silvertown, named after Hugh and his older brother, Stephen William Silver.

Charles Hancock, of the West Ham Gutta Percha company, joined forces with the Silver brothers in 1860, and together they took out a patent for insulating materials. The India Rubber Gutta Percha and Telegraph Works Company was born. Hugh Silver gave the name 'Ebonite' to the

Enderfield *Abbey Lodge*

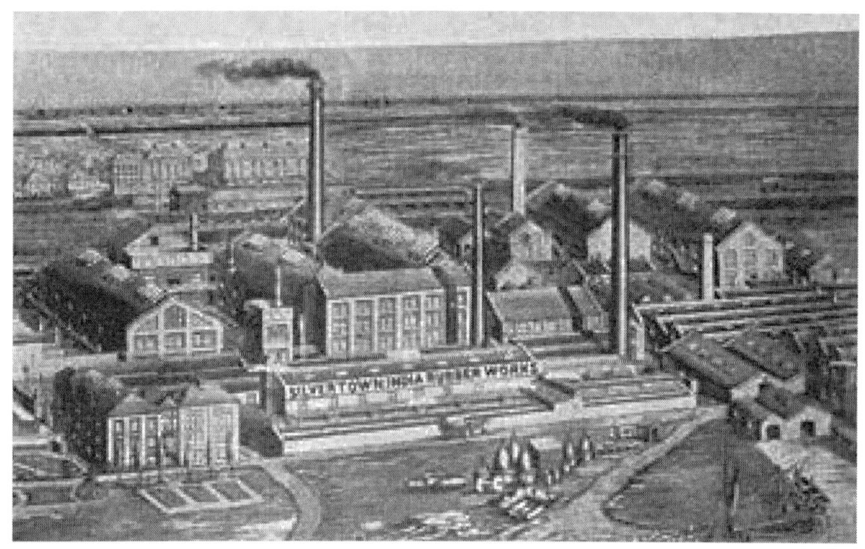

Two views of Silvertown India Rubber Works

substance used extensively in the manufacture of electrical apparatus. Ebonite is manufactured through the vulcanisation of india rubber. The raw materials of india rubber and sulphur came into the country via the London docks, and favoured the location of Silvertown. Gutta-percha is a tough material, made of the coagulated milk juice of the Gutta-percha tree, a native species of South-east Asia. With the combined products of ebonite and india rubber, the newly-formed company entered the field of submarine cable manufacture. The first cable manufactured and laid by the company was for the Submarine Telegraph Company in 1865, running from Dover to Cap Gris-Nez in northern France. This was followed by a cable in 1867, linking Havana, Cuba, and Punta Rassa, Florida. The company owned a wharf on the Thames, from where its four cable-laying ships sailed all over the world. The cable ships, one of which was CS Silvertown, were kept busy laying cables along the west coast of Africa and in South America. CS Silvertown was the largest ship afloat at the time, with the single exception of Brunel's Great Eastern.

In October 1882, Hugh's older brother, Stephen William, retired from the partnership and the business was carried on by Hugh and his two eldest sons, Walter Hugh and Stephen Winkworth Silver. In 1883, Hugh was given the Freedom of the City of London, in the Worshipful Company of Loriners (makers of bits and bridles for horses).

By 1887, the Silvertown site occupied 15 acres (ten of which were taken up by workshops), employed 2,800 people and owned a subsidiary in France employing 300 people. In the 1890s, the workshops began producing bicycle tyres and, later, car tyres. From the time of its earliest cable commissions in 1865 to the 1912 laying of Australian cables, the company claimed to have laid more than 60,000 nautical miles of cable in all continents. As well as submarine cables, the Silvertown works also made a great variety of rubber balls, including tennis balls. In 1900, they manufactured 600,000 india rubber tennis balls and many more gutta-percha golf balls. Other rubber articles produced were tennis shoes, rubber boots, billiard table cushions, waterproof capes and rubber gloves. Domestic bliss! Ebonite articles produced included buttons, combs, paper-knives, thimbles, and 'scores of fancy articles'.

By 1923, the works employed 4,000 people and covered an area of 17 acres. The company was subsumed into the Goodrich Rubber Company in 1934, but the factory was badly bombed in the Second World War. The site was sold and redeveloped as the Thameside Industrial Estate in the 1960s.

It is interesting to note that the West Ham Gutta Percha Company operated from works in Abbey Lane, West Ham. West Ham lay in the ancient half hundred of Becontree, which belonged to Barking Abbey, the oldest and richest nunnery in England. The Abbey was founded in 670, dedicated to the Virgin Mary, and the nuns belonged to the Benedictine order. At the dissolution of the monasteries in 1539, the Abbey surrendered to the Crown. All that remains today is a tower within the parish church. I don't think we had an Abbey in Chislehurst, but it is entirely possible that the Colonel and his aspiring young wife called their new home after the ancient Abbey near the fount of their fortune.

I wish I could find a portrait of the Colonel; I think he must have been quite a character to be in charge of underwater cables, rubber gloves and tennis balls! He also raised and equipped the 9th (Silvertown) Essex Rifle Volunteer Corps, the command of which he held for thirty years. He began as Captain Commandant in February 1860, rising to Lieutenant Colonel by November 1863. His fourth son, Frank, became a 2nd Lieutenant in 1877. In 1882, Hugh patented the breech-loading firearm. By 1891, he is listed as 'retired'. Unlike other grandees of the road at the time, he doesn't seem to have had a second London address. He was a member of the Institute of Civil Engineers but is not listed as a member of any particular club.

Two of Hugh's sons were educated at Oxford– Frank, mentioned above, who matriculated in 1879, aged 21, and fifth son, Alexander, who went up to Exeter College aged 18 in 1883. Seventh son Ernest Edward Septimus became a medical student, but he died in 1894 in Bournemouth, leaving his effects to his older brother, third son Hugh William, who was also training to be a doctor. Hugh William became a surgeon and lived in Sydenham. The grave of Ernest is in St Nicholas churchyard; the headstone nestles just beside the church on the west flank, leaning rather awkwardly. Abbey Lodge is inscribed on the stone, along with the record of the death of his youngest (half) sister, Honor, in 1963. Hugh's eldest son predeceased him, dying in Brighton in 1903, aged only 53; he left his estate to his friend, Charles Woodbridge. Sixth son Edgar emigrated to Australia and was a clerk in Melbourne, most likely with the family business. He enlisted with the Commonwealth forces in 1914; he survived the war and died in New South Wales in 1936. William Humphrey, Hugh's last child, was killed in action in the Great War in France, and was buried in Cambrin Military Cemetery in June 1918; he was 34. He is not listed on the Chislehurst war memorial, as the family had moved away before the war.

When the Colonel retired from the direct running of the Silvertown business, his activities with the regiment seem to have been important enough to him to register that as his occupation. The 1901 census has him at Abbey Lodge with a smaller retinue – only his daughter Jessie, from his first marriage (a spinster of 40), and his three children from his second wife (in their teens). He was 75. By the 1911 census, he is at 11 Burstock Road, Putney, apparently a small house of only four rooms. This is hard to believe, but no servants are listed, just his daughter Honor, aged 30, and his son, Hugh Cornish, an electrical engineer. Looking at Google Earth, it is a period property, a neat Victorian terrace with at least four storeys. It's far more likely that the enumerator didn't complete the form correctly. I just don't believe he had fallen on hard times; the company was at the height of its success but I never found a will to determine his final wealth. Hugh died the following year, in March 1912, aged 86; he is buried in Richmond Cemetery.

Stamford Hill, 1882
The first aerial photograph of London, taken by Cecil Shadbolt

14. Beechcroft

1880 - 1892
Cecil Victor Shadbolt: Up, Up and Away!

Browsing the 1881 census, I nearly overlooked the name George Shadbolt at Beechcroft. I'm so glad I paused for a moment; something about that name was familiar. It led to a real tale of distinction, but also to a story with a tragic ending. Shadbolt was the name I had seen associated with the tale of the 'Rector takes to the Air' in Dorothy McCall's *Patchwork of the History of Chislehurst*. Dorothy, like me, had wonderful moments of discovery: she received a communication from a lady in Tunbridge Wells who ended her letter, 'I saw the balloon go up with the faithful hanging on to Canon Murray's coat tails, in the vain attempt to prevent him going in it!' This refers to an escapade above the skies of London, of Canon Murray, with one Cecil Victor Shadbolt, who was a local amateur photographer and balloonist. Keen readers of local history will recall the story also told by Tom Bushell and Arthur Battle.

I couldn't let this go, and delved further into the life of Cecil. Photography was in the family; his father George – although cited as a merchant in the census – was a member of the council of the Photographic Society and had his work displayed in the *Photographic Journal* in 1859, the year that Cecil was born. There were six Shadbolt sons in total, and one daughter. Cecil was the fifth born child. George had his own firm of timber merchants and Cecil subsequently worked with him at Billiter Street, EC1. George was one of the founders of the Photographic Society in London, in 1853. In such a home atmosphere, it's no wonder that Cecil quickly mastered both the art and science of photography. By the age of 23, he had won a number of medals at exhibitions held all over the country. His most successful year was probably 1882, when six of his photographs were exhibited at the Photographic Society of Great Britain.

Cecil's brother Percy is worthy of a brief note in an unrelated industry. In the 1870s, Percy joined his uncle in the firm Coles, Shadbolt & Co, when the company was erecting a new Portland cement works at Harefield, Middlesex. Percy became joint managing partner. Coles, Shadbolt & Co figured among the firms that amalgamated in 1911 to form the British Portland Cement Manufacturers.

Another older brother, Sidney, trained as a lawyer but wrote a novel,

Moonbeam Tangle, and, rather differently, historical books on the Afghan Wars of 1878.

Undoubtedly Cecil's major achievement was his photograph of Stamford Hill, taken from a free-floating balloon. This appears to be the earliest extant picture of the earth which is truly vertical – that is, taken from the air. For this image alone, Shadbolt has a place in the history of photography. 'Up to the time of undertaking the trip in question, it had never been my good fortune to meet with any satisfactory photograph taken from a balloon.' His opportunity occurred on the bank holiday of June 1882. He went to Alexandra Palace, where he met a Mr Barker, who owned the balloon Reliance. Cecil attached his camera 'by means of an arrangement I had rigged-up in order to enable the instrument to be fixed at any desired angle from the side of the car.' His third exposure was the most successful. For technical readers: his camera was fitted with a simple flap, enabling a shutter speed of one-quarter to half a second. I'm not going to pretend I understand any of that, but perhaps keen photographers will!

When just over Stamford Hill, at an altitude of 2,000 feet, the picture recorded the junction of the Enfield track of the Great Eastern Railway with the Tottenham and Hampstead line. The photograph shows the roofs of houses lined up with regularity, one beside the other, their gardens all alike and of the same size. Cecil had produced the first recognisable picture from cloud land. The Photographic News remarked: 'although not quite equal to Nadir's picture of the roofs of Paris, Mr Shadbolt's view is undoubtedly the best specimen of balloon photography which has been done in this country.'

Fired with such early success, Cecil enthusiastically continued his ballooning activities, buying a new craft, the Sunbeam, in partnership with William Dale. In 1884, a third balloon, Monarch, was launched. It was from this craft that the image of Shadbolt and Dale is taken. It was from Monarch that Cecil made his most successful aerial photographs, using them to illustrate lantern slide lectures.

Photography was inextricably linked to his other passion, the church. A committed Christian, Cecil was active in his faith, first as a Sunday school teacher; then, from 1886, as one of the secretaries of the Western Kent Sunday School Union. It seems that he was primarily associated with Bromley Congregational Church. For twelve years, he was the 'indefatigable' Sunday school teacher here in Lubbock Road. All references to his life paint a picture of him as a reliable, if introverted, young man, modest and quiet

Cecil Shadbolt and William Dale, 1884

Shadbolt's balloon at Alexandra Palace (above), and (on 29 June 1892) at Crystal Palace (below)

of speech and habit.

During the 1880s, he travelled in Palestine and fifteen of his 'photogravures' were published in Walks in Palestine, by Henry A. Harper. I have a copy of the book (naturally), and the photographs must have been ground-breaking for their day, close-up images of life in unknown territory.

Cecil was a sport balloonist. He made 67 ascents in total, many from Chislehurst, and was considered one of Britain's most experienced balloonists. The contemporary description in the Bromley Record of the ascent with Canon Murray makes lovely reading. 'The Latest Novelty in Ballooning! - on Saturday afternoon May 18th 1888 [Dorothy McCall got her dates muddled; she said it was 1899, but I'm afraid Shadbolt was dead by then] in splendid spring weather Mr Cecil Shadbolt, the well-known amateur aeronaut, accompanied by the Rev F H Murray, Mr Richard White of Chislehurst and Mr T Haywood of Sidcup made a balloon ascent from the Rectory Field. A charge for admission to the field was made, Cray Valley Hospital was to benefit by £19. The balloon slowly filled up and the Rector carefully donned a warm woollen cardigan. There actually wasn't enough gas and Mr Haywood, the editor of the Kentish Times had to get out. At 3.40 p.m. the balloon ascended to 1,000 feet and the Rector was able to look down and recognise the crossroads on the Common below. Apparently, a message was received on the ground from the balloon. [How? This was way before the days of mobile phones. Loud hailer, I assume!] "All right in Eclipse balloon, crossing Chislehurst at 1,000 feet altitude." Unfortunately, there was a problem in gaining enough height and the crew had to jettison nearly the whole of their ballast, they found themselves falling midst a large cluster of houses by the Custom House Railway Station, they just cleared the chimney pots and landed safely in a field adjoining a coal yard in Beckton Road. In a few minutes, a crowd, containing a large proportion of "roughs" gathered in the field and pressed forward, catching hold of the ropes on every side, attempted to pull the balloon down by force. The bag being half full of gas heaved and swayed dangerously. One of the aeronauts got his feet entangled in the netting and the balloon making a sudden lurch in the opposite direction he was carried up head downwards several feet in the air but was extricated without injury. The crowd had by this time swelled to five thousand and the police were unable to cope. We are told the Rector's clerical hat was squashed flat as a pancake. Several large rents appeared in the silk, cords were broken and much other damage was done to the apparatus. Several other officers appeared on the scene and with their assistance the balloon was rescued. The coal yard owner demanded half a year's rent of his premises to assure their release, though this was reduced slightly in the end but the party were finally able to depart and return to Chislehurst via cart to Canning Town. The aeronauts arrived home not much worse for wear but with a clearer idea of what mob law is than they ever had before.'

Cecil saw no danger in ballooning, provided proper precautions were taken. Like most aeronauts, he had many a rough-and-tumble descent, but always escaped anything of the nature of a serious accident. Indeed, while others had to be lifted from the car, he escaped with the merest shaking, weak and delicate though he seemed to be. He absolutely revelled in these aerial trips and was very fond of teasing his friends, recounting to them on a dull and rainy day the beautiful weather he had experienced above the clouds.

Cecil reduced the practice of ballooning as far as possible to a science and sometimes, to show his friends how much control one could have over a balloon, given favourable conditions, he would ascend and descend following the conformations of the ground by careful management of ballast and gas check.

His insouciance was not to last. Shadbolt's untimely death was both dramatic and tragic.Who's Who of Ballooning reported the death of Cecil Shadbolt with William Dale (Cecil actually financed Dale in the balloon business). Dale was no novice in terms of ballooning, having made more than 200 flights from Crystal Palace by 1888. However, their last ascent, on 29 June 1892, quickly ended in tragedy. At 5.45 pm, Captain Dale shouted, 'Let's go!' and the balloon rose quickly, reaching an altitude of 600 feet within minutes. The crowds of spectators were horrified to see it collapse. Apparently, the balloon had had several previous owners – including Baden-Powell – and had been considered 'un-airworthy' years before being 'rejuvenated' as two balloons. It had sustained a serious rupture on its previous flight and had received extensive repairs just before inflation. The balloon, newly repaired by Mrs Dale, ruptured at considerable height before her eyes. Deprived of its buoyancy, the balloon came down like a rag. The occupants could be seen vainly struggling, madly throwing out ballast bags and everything that they could, to lighten the car. They even wrenched buttons from their clothing. Dale died soon after impact, but his son, also on board, survived. Cecil died nine days later at Norwood Cottage Hospital, from internal injuries.

His eulogy was printed in *Walks in Palestine*: 'Mr Shadbolt's death was as beautiful as his life had been, on awakening from unconsciousness with all the pain of that poor shattered body there was not once complaint nor impatience, there was even in his hours of fitful sleep, prayer that he should be taken out of his suffering when God saw fit. At length this gifted, cultured happy servant of Christ with calm and confident mind passed quietly and peacefully to his eternal home.' This eulogy was a typically Victorian piece, reported by the Religious Tract Society. I hate to be a detractor, but other reports comment that he never regained consciousness. He was described in his obituary as a 'very gentle perfect knight' to the young and to the weak, a man who feared God and had no other fear.

The Times had followed the medical reports after the accident, and the circumstances of his death were sufficiently sensational to attract widespread interest. The jury of the Coroners' enquiry returned a verdict of 'Death from accidental causes', and added that, in their opinion, the filling of the balloon was properly carried out and that no one was to blame for the matter. The funeral was held on 13 July, and Cecil Shadbolt was interred in Norwood Cemetery in the presence of many sorrowing friends. Reverend Fleming made a feeling reference to him at Christ Church on the Sunday after his death.

Cecil's mother had died in the winter the year before Cecil met with his fate, but George lived into ripe old age, dying in 1901. The family left Beechcroft soon after the accident, and it subsequently became one of the many temporary parsonages of Christ Church. It is now the site of Lubbock Court.

Beechcroft being demolished

Claverley

15. Claverley

1878 - 1902
Sir Robert W. Perks MP
Motorways, Methodism and La Manche

Researching Claverley brought to my attention the deep-seated legacy of Methodism in Chislehurst. The first occupant of the original 'Claverley' (it is now much altered) was Robert William Perks, a very significant character in the history of Methodism in this country. Sadly, Sir Robert did not live in Lubbock Road at the height of his success, as he truly was distinctive. He attended Kingswood School near Bath, and moved to Eldon House, Clapham, for his final years. Mathematics was his forte and geology his hobby. At King's College, London, he took most of the college prizes, and his time there was a brilliant one, gaining honours in Classics, English and Modern Languages. He joined De Jersey Micklem, a City law firm practicing in Gresham Street. His articles cost £300. In his four years of training, he received no remuneration and had to support himself through journalism, writing for the London Quarterly Review.

He was a very hard worker and often worked late into the night, but he also lived by his own rule to 'never to be in bed of a morning after five'. To enforce this rule, he invented an ingenious machine: a long glass tube filled with water, balanced over his head and attached to an alarm. At the desired hour, the alarm sounded, but if Robert did not leap from his bed, the descending weight of the clock destroyed the balance of the tube and water poured down on his sleepy head!

Robert specialised in railway law and became the legal adviser to the Metropolitan Railway; in 1901, he became Chairman of the Metropolitan District Railway. He made his fortune in property investment, buying into the large developing estates in the thriving suburbs, and reselling at a profit. In 1876, he went into business for himself, along with Mr Henry Hartley Fowler (later Lord Wolverhampton) and Mr Charles Corser, from offices in Leadenhall Street.

Robert married in 1878, and the family home in Highbury was broken up, as four of his sisters and his father had passed away. Robert had met his wife, Edith Mewburn, when visiting a school friend from his Clapham days, William Mewburn, the son of a Methodist layman. The president of the Wesleyan Conference conducted the wedding ceremony, a Wesleyan minister's son was best man and the bride's health was proposed by Robert's

Robert William Perks MP

business partner. I can't imagine her health was toasted with alcohol, given the strict religious observances of the gathering!

The newlyweds made their home in Chislehurst and Robert had Claverley built for what was to become a family of five: four daughters – Gertrude, Mildred, Edith and Margaret, each born two years apart – and finally, in 1892, a son, Robert Mewburn. The name Claverley is derived from Robert senior's maternal grandmother, Elizabeth Claverley. Robert cherished her memory with some affection, and family folklore has it that she was descended from stiff Jacobean stock.

Lady Perks took pride in her charming homes; their city home was at Kensington Gardens, and was crowded with books, paintings, engravings and all sorts of curiosities indicative of cultured taste. She was described as gracious and tactful whether entertaining prominent statesmen or humble Methodists.

For fifteen years, Robert led, to use his own words, 'the regular, quiet, unostentatious life which a hard-working professional man crowded up with business must lead.' 'Methodism, my business and my home absorbed all my attention.' He certainly devoted much of his time to the 'handsome Gothic church' here in Chislehurst and, in 1881, he and Sir George Chubb were joint stewards of the church. Robert worked at the little Sunday school in Widmore Road and gave assistance at Sunday night prayer meetings. Apparently, he and his devoted wife were 'ever ready with sympathy and service.'

In 1892, Sir Robert was elected Liberal Member of Parliament for the constituency of Louth in Lincolnshire. He retained the seat in 1895 and again in 1906. Robert was to be associated with the original plans for a cross-Channel rail link, a design for a circular road around London and, most particularly, with the fundraising for Methodist Central Hall, Westminster.

Undoubtedly his finest hour came in association with the Twentieth Century Fund and the Methodist brotherhood. This took up nearly three years of this life and was, he said, 'the most arduous, anxious, and successful religious and philanthropic enterprise in which I was ever engaged'. A book, The Making of the Million, by John Ackworth, is dedicated with honest and hearty admiration to R.W. Perks Esq, MP, the originator of that 'unique and wonderful movement', the Wesleyan Twentieth Century Fund. The fund was first set up in Hull in 1898, as a mechanism for fundraising. The aims were set high, £300,000 for the purchase of sites and the erection of chapels, Sunday schools and mission halls; £200,000 for educational work; £100,000 for foreign missionary work, and a further £100,000 for home missionary work, including temperance work; £250,000 for the purchase of a suitable site in London for building a monumental Connexional Building; and £50,000 for the development of a children's home, to save all children of Methodist and Nonconformist parentage from the workhouse.

People donated one guinea to be recorded on the Historic Roll and, by 1899, £17,945 had already been donated. A site for the monumental building was identified by Perks, the 40,000 acre site of the Royal Aquarium in Westminster, to be purchased at £4 per sq ft. By the meeting of December 1900, the Twentieth Century Fund stood at £423,696, and it was agreed to open a list of 1,000 donations of 100 guineas to supplement this amount. By 1901, the fund had reached £965,019. The Fund was wound up in 1904, having reached its targets. The whole scheme seemed to have germinated in Perks's own brain: quite simply – a million guineas from a million Methodists.

However, I have to acknowledge that Perks was mostly living in Kensington at this point – or another home in New Romney, which he also called Claverley – so I cannot really claim the greatest distinction of his career to have emanated from Lubbock Road. I can say, though, that it most certainly germinated from here.

1902-1912
Helen Craggs, Suffragette: At Home with the Pethick-Lawrences

I was looking at the next resident of Claverley after Sir Robert Perks, and came across Sir John Craggs, M.V.O. That wasn't a suffix I had come across before. It means he was a Member of the Royal Victorian Order, a personal gift of the Monarch, an honour for some form of personal or community service. In Sir John's case, it was the latter, as a chartered accountant with Price Waterhouse & Co; he had been the honorary secretary of King Edward's Hospital Fund from its foundation in 1897.

A member of the Carlton Club, listed in The Peerage of the United Kingdom as a 'philanthropist', and with his sons educated at Charterhouse, Craggs was a pillar of the Establishment for sure. Distinctive and fortunate in the circle he kept. How could he have known that the world he understood was about to be challenged, disturbed and radically affected by the actions of his second daughter and, indeed, to a more limited extent, also by those of his wife!

This genteel family had been living at Glen Druid, on the corner of Southill Road and Yester Road, until 1902. A burgeoning family, of six children – two boys and four girls – they probably needed more space. Lady Craggs, whose Christian name was Helen, was to have two more children after the move to Claverley. She was a suffragette, a member of the Conservative and Unionist Women's Franchise Association. As the name suggests, this was a women's suffrage organisation open to members on the political right. They supported the 'extension of the franchise to all duly qualified women'. Their activities were not exactly militant: they ran two newspapers and attended marches. It may have been the lady's genteel approach to women's rights that caused her second daughter – also called Helen – to respond in a rather more reactionary way to the issue. Lady Craggs may have rued the day she told her namesake about the cause.

Young Helen had been educated at Roedean and returned there as a member of staff, teaching Physics, Chemistry, Gymnastics and Dance. Somewhat pompously to us, her father had refused to allow her to study medicine. However, this was not uncommon: in the early twentieth century, women who wanted to study medicine received a great deal of objection from men in the profession, and the general attitude in society towards women doctors was very negative. Helen was obviously a victim of that culture. No wonder she turned to drastic action to promote the cause of women.

She must have had some level of respect for her father's wishes, as, in order to avoid embarrassing Sir John, she campaigned for the Women's Social and Political Union as 'Miss Millar'. The WSPU was the leading militant organisation campaigning for the vote, founded by the Pankhurst family in 1903. It was a women-only organisation, allied largely with the Independent Labour Party. Mother and daughter seemed on a collision course from the start, despite their shared vision.

Helen sold suffragette postcards, rang the bell to summon audiences to meetings, and chalked up announcements of meetings at the Peckham by-election of 1908. By 1910, she was an organiser and working full time for the Union, being paid 25 shillings a week. She left the family home in Lubbock Road to live in Bloomsbury. While she was campaigning in Manchester, she met Emmeline Pankhurst's young son, Henry. He was to die in January 1910, from paralysis from an inflamed spinal cord, and Helen was at his bedside during the last few weeks of his fatal illness.

By February of that year Helen, was back on the militant trail, organising a campaign in Brixton. She was in Hampstead in March but imprisoned in Holloway, after taking part in a window-smashing campaign. She went on hunger strike but was released. She earned her particular distinction in the early hours of 13 July 1912, when she was arrested carrying all the paraphernalia for arson. PC Godden, of the Oxfordshire Constabulary, apprehended one of two women who were standing near the wall of Nuneham House, the county residence of Lewis Harcourt, a leading anti-women's franchise campaigner in the Cabinet. The constable impounded a basket and a satchel, which together contained a bottle and two cans of methylated spirits, four tapers, nine pick-locks, twelve fire lighters, a hammer, an electric torch and a piece of American cloth smeared with some 'sticky substance'. In the bag belonging to the apprehended Helen was a note, addressed to 'Sir' which said, 'I myself have taken part in every peaceful method of propaganda and petition....but have been driven to realise that it has all been of no avail, so now I....have done something drastic'.

Helen subsequently received nine months' imprisonment but was released after a hunger strike of eleven days. Bail was set at £1,000, paid for by her horrified father.

It was time for a parting of the family ways; Helen moved to Dublin to train as a midwife and, in 1914, married Alexander McCrombie, a GP from Aberdeen who had been working in the East End of London. Sir John and Lady Craggs did not attend the wedding; the charitable among us will note it was 1914 and she was in Ireland, but there may just have been another reason.

Helen's medical ambitions were realised in the form of her training as a pharmacist and working alongside her husband as a dispenser. Helen and Alex had two children, but after his death Helen ran a jigsaw-making business to support herself and her family. She emigrated to Canada with her daughter after the Second World War and, by quite a turn of events, re-married in 1957, to Frederick Pethwick-Lawrence, the widower of Emmeline Pankhurst. He may have been a baron, elevated to the Peerage in 1945 – having acted as Leader of the Opposition to the wartime coalition government – but I don't think it was quite the distinction her parents had anticipated for her, back in their Lubbock Road days!

16. The Great War

1914-1918
A change in the road - hospitals and heroines

Abbey Lodge is a remarkable survivor of a bygone age. It's incredible to think that it was the First World War that actually saved her, and that, amazingly, the Second World War did not fell her either, unlike so many other Victorian mansions in the area, destroyed by incendiary devices.

As early as 1903, Abbey Lodge is listed as 'vacant' in Kelly's Directory. The Victorian era had slipped into the reign of King Edward VII, but peaceful the world was not. Sir John Lubbock was warning the world of the rising aggression of Germany and founded the Albert Committee to sue for peaceful relations with our Continental neighbours. A meeting was called locally by a Dr Allan, to consider the advisability of forming a Voluntary Aid Detachment in the neighbourhood. Kent 60 was set up in 1912, under commandant Miss Alston.

Sir John Lubbock, latterly Lord Avebury, died in May 1913, and with

Abbey Lodge 1914

him passed an altogether more peaceful era than the one that was about to unfold. The war was undoubtedly a significant turning point in the history of the road, but in terms of the survival of its heritage not an altogether disastrous one.

In August 1914, Kent 60 worked hard to prepare the necessary equipment for a hospital, and members were able to gain practical experience at the Cray Valley Hospital. As the crisis on the Continent was rapidly brought home, Lubbock Road began its new role. Orders to mobilise came very quickly at midnight on 13 October. Christ Church Hall had 25 beds ready by 6 a.m., and 33 wounded Belgian soldiers arrived at 9 a.m. The more minor casualties were sent to Coed-bel, where Miss Fox, the headmistress, lent her school's sanatorium to the effort, with eight beds. Mr Straus from Hatton Cottage helped with the accounts, and Mrs Helen Oldendorft of Beechbrook was a member of the committee. I'd like to think that the road's 21st century neighbours would come together in the same way today.

After two days, instructions were received to prepare for more patients, and it was at that time that Abbey Lodge was equipped as a hospital. Thirty more Belgians arrived on 17 October. Curiously, according to the Red Cross archives, 'Abbey Lodge was obtained rent free for a year via William Willett from Mr Erskine of Ryde. The initial difficulties of preparing this hospital were great as the house had long been empty, but it is adaptable for

Waiting for the wounded outside Chislehurst Station

Commerative plaque inside Abbey Lodge

Abbey Lodge

Beatrix Batten with nurses and wounded soldiers outside Christ Church

Wounded men inside Christ Church

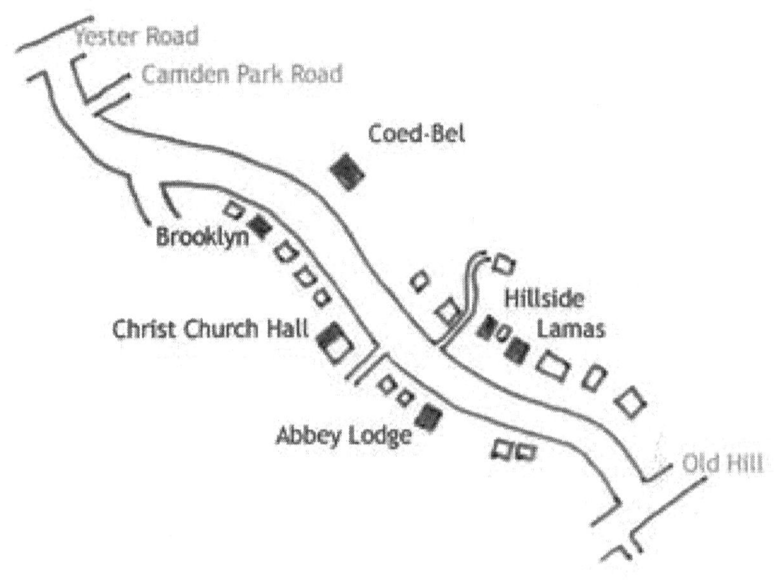

Red Cross hospital sites in Lubbock Road

Outside Brooklyn Red Cross Hospital

The Pole sisters, (left to right), Gladys, Hilda, Lily and Muriel.

Rev. William Pole

Wounded soldiers at the gates to Lamas

use being built on institutional lines.' We know Colonel Silver was long gone, but had no one else moved in? Had the Colonel built the house thinking to run it as a school, convent or some other institution? I can find no reference to the like. Willett was the builder who had purchased Camden Park from Nathaniel Strode in 1893. He had designs for the Park to be turned into a large housing estate but had been thwarted by the Metropolitan Commons Act and the legal weight of Alexander Travers Hawes and the Commons Conservators. Was this Willett doing his public duty and negotiating the new use for Abbey Lodge, or did he have the long game in mind? After all, property developers always have an eye to profit margins and speculative development. Abbey Lodge was, after all, a very large site, running as it did then all the way down to the stream. Willett became a victim of the Spanish 'flu that killed so many during and after the war, but he wasn't to know that in 1914.

The photographic scene of motor cars, queuing up at Chislehurst Station to transport the wounded depicts the sense of urgency there. Knowing how many steps there are to descend and ascend to get from the platforms to the road, I remain perplexed as to how they physically got the wounded off the northbound trains, though I imagine the trains were switched to station side track.

Christ Church 'hospital' moved further down the road, to a house called

Brooklyn, where Ross Court stands now, lent by Mr Acton Garle for the winter. Beatrix was to give a lifetime's service to the Red Cross, becoming County Director for Kent and received the C.B.E. from the Queen. There is a memorial to her in Christ Church.

Lamas too, became a VAD hospital, being an auxiliary of the Ontario Hospital at Orpington, operating until 1919. Hillside, next door, was also utilised from September 1918 to March 1919.

Reverend Pole, the wartime incumbent of Christ Church, had given his parish room at 'great inconvenience', but four of his daughters rose to the nursing challenge with fortitude. I enjoyed researching the lives of 'the Pole sisters', though my internet now constantly bombards me with less-than-salubrious images of pole dancers!

According to *Kent's Care for the Wounded*, 'At the beginning there was the usual half contemptuous chaff, even sneers, at hospital amateurs, but amateur assistance is drawn from the most intelligent and best classes of the community with a sense of responsibility and a voluntary desire to accomplish a purpose.' Each VAD member was given a note which read: 'You have to perform tasks which will need your courage, your energy, your patience, your humility, your determination to overcome all difficulties. It will be your duty not only to set an example of discipline and perfect steadiness of character, but also to maintain the most courteous relations with those whom you are helping in this great struggle. Sacrifices may be asked of you. Give generously and wholeheartedly, grudging nothing, but remembering that you are giving because your Country needs your help.' The Pole sisters – Lily, 31, Muriel, 20, Hilda, 21, and Gladys, 18 – did this to the letter; Lily even rose to be Quartermaster under Miss Batten's command. Gladys recalls that her 21st birthday was spent peeling potatoes and skinning rabbits in the kitchen of Abbey Lodge. Even though the grand house was wholly used as a hospital, the VAD nurses were never allowed to use the main staircase, being told in no uncertain terms to use the back stairs (which the current owner confirms still exist).

The Pole family have an interesting heritage. William Pole was awarded the third Order of the Rising Sun for his work in establishing Japan's railway system. One of his sons, another William, was a famous producer of Shakespeare at the old Globe Theatre, London. The eldest son, the Reverend George Henry Pole, Cambridge-educated – with nine years of missionary and theological college experience from Osaka, Japan, behind him – arrived with his family at Christ Church, aged 53, in 1902. He was

Beatrix Batten

Kent 60 Voluntary Aid Detachment, Chislehurst

vicar until 1917 and died in Bromley in 1929. He had two other daughters amongst the VAD recruits, and one surviving son, two other sons having died young. It seems that the girls continued a life of service after the war; Hilda became a missionary, returning to Japan via Canada in 1929. Another sister, Dorothy, worked as missionary in West Africa. They lived well into their eighties, and Hilda died at the age of 90 back in the UK. Their brother Reginald, a Cambridge Prizeman, emigrated to Florida on account of his asthma. A friend of Rupert Brooke, he became a dramatist, poet, composer, director and actor, as well as lecturing on philosophy. In Palm Springs, he married actress, Helen Taggart (later Mrs Lloyd Wright), and was friends with Charlie Chaplin.

Sergeant Philip Gibson from Camden Hill, Lieutenant Gerald Harwood of the Rookery, Second Lieutenant James Morum of Seven Trees, Major Frederick Oldendorft of Beechbrook, and Second Lieutenant Peter Wood of Camden Lodge, all died in the war, taking the death toll of Lubbock Road resident sons to five. Private Walter Piper, the gardener from Kincraig (employed by long-standing Swedish resident Alfred Peherson), was another casualty. Their stories are told by Yvonne Auld. Yvonne also recounts the story of Margaret Birkett, a night nurse at Brooklyn, subsequently on the day shift at Abbey Lodge. She was taken ill whilst on duty and died on 16 October 1914, aged only 25. She was allegedly the first Red Cross nurse on home service to have died at her post. Two recuperating soldiers from Brooklyn saluted her burial wreaths at the graveside.

Perhaps, for counterbalance, it is worth recording that all five sons of Robert Raikes, solicitor, who were raised at Enderfield (next door to Abbey Lodge, now flats) fought for the duration of the war and survived. Not only did they survive but all were awarded the D.S.O. for meritorious and distinguished service; two brothers received the M.C. I suspect service was in their genes; their grandfather, also Robert, had founded the concept of Sunday schools in Gloucestershire. Another survivor was John Francis Yeatman, from 22 Lubbock Road, an unmarried accountant who enlisted in the Army Service Corps and was immediately promoted to Staff Sergeant Major in June 1915. Wilfred and Gordon Wood were also survivors, along with the Vinson boys from Raggleswood.

17. Seven Trees (originally Rosedale)

1874 - 1939
A Chemist, a Peripatetic Family and Refugees from Prague

Seven Trees has a very significant place in the history of the road, even in the history of the nation. It began as a family home but during the Second World War, it became a place of sanctuary for children a very long way from their families. The fact that it took on an institutional role is possibly the reason it has survived in a form not too dissimilar to that of the 1870s, when it was built. Now a much-loved family home again, it is a pleasure to see this grand old lady spruced up, and to acknowledge her place as the keeper of a special story.

I have been fortunate with my research on several occasions, and having access to the original indenture – the transaction between Nathaniel Strode and the first owners of this plot of land – was one such stroke of fortune. My erstwhile benefactor, Dave Miller, the self-styled wheeler-dealer, who has procured so many Camden Park indentures from eBay, showed me the document. I was in turn able to show to the current owner, Amanda, who in her turn gave me several leads to the past.

The indenture reveals the sale of the land from Strode to two gentlemen, G. Lethbridge and William Constable. George Lethbridge was a Scottish-born architect who commenced independent practice in London in 1870. Seven Trees, as we know it now, may well have been his design. The house appears on early maps as 'Rosedale', and from residential directories I learned that the first occupant was John Hugill, in 1874. Hugill was described as a 'druggist' in the 1881 census, but this is no more incriminating than his being a chemist and lozenge maker. He was originally from Whitby, but married his wife Esther in London. They began married life in Edmonton, where their twin daughters were born. I can understand the need for a substantial home when I tot up the total number of children born to the couple: after the twins came John, Arthur, George, Louisa, Thomas and Francis. Francis, the youngest, was eight when they came to Rosedale.

John died in 1900, and life must have taken on a lonely air for Esther: the 1901 census has her home alone with only two house parlour maids and a useful maid. At this point, I was lucky to get information from Amanda, who had taken an interest in her house history when she moved in. Once again, the all-knowing vicar, Michael Adams, had been the provider of contacts. He pointed Amanda in the direction of the grand-daughter of the next owner of Rosedale, who still lived on the land, so to speak – in Rosedale Cottage in Lower Camden.

William Morum bought the house in 1907 for the princely sum of £2,200. Would that were the case today! Apparently, he spent a similar amount on repairs. Perhaps the Hugills had done no maintenance over the previous 30 years, and one imagines it was time for electric light and upgraded sanitation. The Morums had three children at that time: James, aged ten, Gwen, aged eight, and baby Francis; another child, Kathleen, was born later. I am grateful to the diligent records acquired by Yvonne Auld, which informed me that James was a victim of the Great War. The family seems to have been somewhat nomadic: 1911 sees the family living in Sidcup, so those repairs must have necessitated living elsewhere for what looks like four years at least! William was a shipping agent, with offices in the Clock Tower Works on the High Street in Lewisham; the four children were born in Sidcup, except for James, who was born in South Africa. William and his wife, Florence, were also born in South Africa (Queenstown in the Eastern Cape Province). William's parents had settled there in the 1860's.

The family were living at Rosedale in July 1916, when James was killed in action. He is remembered at Sucrerie Military Cemetery, Colincamps, on the Somme. He was only 20, and had been an undergraduate at Cambridge when war broke out. His education points to wealth – or, at the very least, ambition – in the family; he had been privately educated at Merton Court in Sidcup and then Wellington College.

James's death was the first tragedy for the family. The next difficulty was the failure of the business in 1927. There are bankruptcy notices in the London Gazette in February of that year. William kept the stable and gardener's cottage, and asked to keep the name Rosedale, so it seems that at that time, Rosedale became a cottage, and Seven Trees became the name of the 'big house'.

Harrods handled the sale of the house, though it appears they used local agent David Chattell. It was in the archive of the latter that I found the particulars described thus: '10 bedrooms, 3 receptions rooms, Ballroom and Billiard room, tennis court and other lawns. Should specifically appeal to a city man seeking first class residence with good accommodation replete with the latest and approved modern conveniences in a recognised high and healthy residential district. Garden stocked with valuable rock plants.' So those 'repairs' were to bathrooms, and it seems the Morums had been keen gardeners. I wonder how many grand dances were held in that ballroom?

According to Strong's Bromley Directory, the purchaser seems to be have been Alfred Plumbridge Langley. In 1933, the occupant was Morgan Phillips Griffith-Jones, a barrister, who had served as a Major with the Durham Light Infantry in the Great War. He received an O.B.E. for valuable services at the War Office, and became Metropolitan Magistrate. (The house was potentially vacant after the death of Griffith-Jones, in May 1939).

The fortunes of Seven Trees are indelibly linked to the very special role it played next during the Second World War. A story that may be well known to Lubbock Road residents, but perhaps the curious who have seen the bench at the corner of the junction of the road with Old Hill, will be interested to learn more of the bench's relationship with Seven Trees.

The year is 1938. Hitler marches into the Sudetenland, and the plight of the Czechoslovakian Jews is alarming. Small boys and girls lost their parents and found themselves in a Europe boiling over with hatred and cruelty. But there was to be one tiny glimmer of hope. The Barbican Mission to the Jews had a Mission Centre in Prague, which was becoming thronged from morning till night with distressed parents; it was to this mission that the Rev. I.E. Davidson went, in early 1938. His visit was one of ceaseless activity, besieged by hundreds of families eager for an interview, in the hope that children with claims to British nationality (by having been born there or having one British parent), could gain the necessary authority to travel. It was agreed that fifty children could be taken to England, but first permits had to be arranged. (There was at this time an organisation already in existence, whose object was to rescue children from Germany, and later from Austria, but Czechoslovakia had not yet been taken into consideration). There were weeks of delay and that the first fifty permits did eventually come through was, with hindsight, nothing short of a miracle.

The problem of housing the children required further herculean effort. Chislehurst was known to the Mission as having many large houses, although many had apparently been empty for years and were in a hopeless state of dilapidation. That was the rather illuminating comment from Mrs Davidson, reflecting on the changes in domestic housing in the inter-war years. Following the depression in the Thirties, big houses just didn't sell, and were left to go to rack and ruin. It's not apparent from my research that this was the case in Lubbock Road, but when one looks at Camden Lodge, this is the era when it was subdivided into flats. Hillside had already been demolished before 1937, as shown by the aerial photograph taken in that year.

Seven Trees was identified as accommodation that was in every way suitable, but the owners (presumably the beneficiaries of Morgan Phillips) were somewhat capricious, and the purchase went through with extraordinary slowness. The purchase was all but complete when a Lubbock Road resident took up a position of powerful opposition.

I found his letter published in The Bromley Times:

Friday January 20th 1939

Dear Sir

Your readers in the locality will be interested in the following activity protesting against the invasion of foreigners.

The following letter was signed by 31 landlords and residents of Lubbock Road and forwarded to the Council: - "We the undersigned property owners and ratepayers strongly protest to the council against the proposed use of Seven Trees as a home for foreign refugees. It will greatly depreciate the sale value, amenities and rateable value of all the properties in Lubbock Road and adjoining neighbourhood. Both house and garden are wholly unsuitable for such a purpose and quite inadequate for the fifty children and requisite attendants (as quoted in the press). Also, its proximity to London in air raids should receive due consideration and we herewith record our protest against any further proposal to utilise other premises in Lubbock Road for this purpose. We property owners and ratepayers claim the right of protection by the Council of our interests and consider that the residential district of Chislehurst is totally unsuitable for the purpose suggested. "I implore the charitable to have their foreign children in the many large houses well away from expensive London where the kids will enjoy it better and won't trouble or hurt our own nationals. When these children grow up it would give the dictator from their country of origin enough excuse to demand annexation of the country they reside in."

Yours faithfully, Gordon Ivey, Sandy Ridge, Lubbock Road.

However, there were positive neighbours in the road, too. Rev. Davidson addressed a large drawing room meeting at Hatton House by the invitation of Mrs Fehr. The Rev. J.R. Carpenter, of Christ Church, was at the meeting and encouraged help in the form of money and household items, to be sent directly to Rev. Davidson at Lower Camden. It was also helpful that the Chislehurst Refugee Association was actively re-homing children at another large house in the area, Seafield. The leader of Bromley Council was in fact a staunch ally, and took up the matter on behalf of the

Seven Trees

Barbican Mission to the Jews dedicated bench on the corner of Lubbock Road and Old Hill

Rev. I.E.Davidson and Mrs Lucy Davidson with the first group of Czechoslovak refugees

3 year-old Hans Neumann (Beck) with Nicholas Winton

Mission. Rev. Carpenter drew up a petition to the Council and asked all the members of his congregation to sign it, on leaving church on Sunday morning. The motion to restrain the activities of the Mission was defeated, and Seven Trees became the home of the first wave of bewildered children from Prague.

At this juncture, I pondered further on the Barbican Mission, and googled 'rescued children from Prague'. The inevitable Kindertransport web pages came up, and I was struck by the particular story of Nicholas Winton. This gentleman had organised the evacuation of many hundreds of children from Prague, but his story was only revealed by Esther Rantzen in 1988. At the time of writing, Mr Winton was still alive, aged 104, the holder of an M.B.E. from the Queen, and with a proposal for a Nobel Peace Prize on the table. I made contact with the Winton family, enquiring if 'Nicky', as he preferred to be known, had had any dealings with the Davidsons. Amazingly, though he had no recall of Rev. Davidson himself, Nicky clearly recalls putting children onto a flight on 12 January, bound for Croydon Airport. This was the Barbican Mission flight. The particularly famous (and only) photograph of Nicky holding a young child is in fact of little Hans Neumann, (subsequently, Beck) a three-year-old destined for Chislehurst.

As Mrs Lucy Davidson tells in her own story *For a Future and a Hope*, 'At last the day came when Seven Trees was vacant and we were able to move out of the Parish Hall, a huge undertaking simply carrying beds and possessions across the road, but what a joy to be settled in a proper house and such a delightful one.' Not a moment too soon! Rev. Davidson brought a further twelve children out of Prague a week before Hitler marched in.

The accommodation issue immediately became a further problem. Lamas – subsequently St Hugh's Prep School – had become empty, and we come full circle in the story of the road. There was a gymnasium, an annexe for staff bedrooms, nurseries for the little ones, and an excellent garden with a bungalow for a resident gardener. In the main house, there were very large rooms and adequate bathrooms. But the Mission once again had to face the opposition of the neighbours and some of the Council. The leader advised a petition which would thoroughly canvass the neighbours. At many houses, they met coldness and indifference, larger numbers refusing to sign anything. Some signed readily, for the sake of the children; and then there was a real breakthrough, as 'the old gentleman who had been our most bitter opponent had since been largely won over.

Though openly disliking children, he personally told me that our boys were the best behaved he had ever met and rather rashly perhaps added that if he could ever help me at any time he would be pleased to do so.' Lucy made sure his name was the first on the new petition, and the refugee boys were able to move into what became known as 'Mount Zion'. Sir John Lubbock would very likely have approved.

In total, fifty-seven boys and forty-two girls were rescued and cared for by the Mission here in Lubbock Road. There were readers of Cockpit, the magazine of the Chislehurst Society, who queried how they had come to encounter Czechoslovak children at school with them at Edgebury.

Amanda had been doing her own research into this story and had made contact with one of the children, now grown up, Anna Meyer. Anna recalls her memories:

'The boys were housed in Mount Zion and the girls in Seven Trees. The garden at Seven Trees was on three levels, the bottom and the shadier one was mainly used for rough tennis and croquet. It no longer forms part of the property. There was a large garage attached to the house on the Christ Church side, its roof covered in a vine bearing delicious fruit. It looked very tempting but we were not allowed to climb up to retrieve it. The long room at the rear on the left was the dining room and one of the front rooms was "the quiet room", though I suspect it wasn't always quiet. It was nicely furnished and I particularly remember two deckchair-style chairs covered in green velvet.

'Both children's homes were staffed by women and a few men, who worked there for the love of God (and, presumably, children too), plus their bread and board and quite modest pocket money. We called the senior one, a buxom lady with a fine singing voice, "Mother", but having left my own mother behind it took me a while to call her that. The other staff were "Aunties", but there were no "uncles" at Mount Zion.

'The Rev. Davidson travelled extensively throughout the country taking Sunday services and speaking at church gatherings, with the collection coming to the Mission. In addition, his sermons created enough interest to bring in sufficient funds in the form of anything from five-shilling postal orders to sizeable cheques and bequests to run both children's homes.

'On Sunday, 3rd September 1939, we were at the morning service in Christ Church when the vicar announced that war had been declared. There was no school for several months and for a while we had an occasional visit by an English teacher. We, children from 3 to 15, learnt English remarkably quickly, even eventually doing quite well at school.

'After the "phony war", German bombers would cross the Channel flying over Kent on their way to London. Sometimes when they failed to bomb their target they offloaded their bombs over Chislehurst and surrounding areas. On one such occasion when it was considered safer for the girls to sleep in the long tiled hall in Seven Trees rather than in the first-floor dormitories, I disobeyed orders and crept upstairs to my comfortable bed. That night two bombs fell on the garage, an oil bomb which broke as intended and an incendiary bomb, which was to have set the oil alight but stayed intact. The house and all of us were saved, the only damage being the roof of the garage and a lot of oil-soaked mattresses in the hall. I had got used to aircraft noise in the night, woke up and went straight back to sleep again. The bombing of London had started in earnest.

'At a Sunday service at Christ Church at about that time the vicar called for volunteers to join a mission to the many families, (mainly from the East End), who had taken more or less permanent shelter in Chislehurst Caves. My hand must have shot up and so I found myself where I, a 14 year-old girl, should not have been allowed to go, singing hymns to this grey, quiet mass of people who probably understood less of the reason for the war that put them there than we children did who had not long before been breathing the fresh air of above-ground Chislehurst. After all we already had firsthand experience of enmity and war. I cannot convey the smell the Cave dwellers created and had to endure. It lives with me still.

'Some time after the bombing incident all the children were evacuated to a large country house not far from Tiverton in Devon and Seven Trees was used by the Barbican Mission as offices and to lodge the office staff.

'A lifetime later in 1989 we had a happy, if nostalgic, reunion in Seven Trees, some of the "kids" coming from overseas, some bringing husbands or wives and even grown-up children. As far as I know none of us had a criminal record, none had become a millionaire, but all appeared to be living relatively comfortably. Most had made a positive contribution to the country that took them in.

'It seemed fitting to commemorate the Davidsons and the friends of the BMJ in a tangible way so we had a dedicated bench placed at the junction of Lubbock Road and Old Hill.'

Interestingly, William Morum died in May 1941, so he would have known that his former home had fulfilled a profoundly useful role.

St Hugh's School

18. St Hugh's School/Mount Zion

1909 - 1960
Boys and Orphans: Full Circle

Delving into the internet back in 2011, I came across a postcard on eBay of the original building of St Hugh's Boys' Preparatory School, Morland House, in Susan Wood. The school still exists in Oxfordshire, but its staff had never seen an image of its Chislehurst roots nor of the Lubbock Road house into which it moved in 1909. I have enjoyed a rich correspondence with the school registrar and received a copy of a centenary history book.

The school moved to Lamas, necessitated by an increase in numbers to 30 pupils, a mixture of boarders and day pupils. One of the dangers of being a day boy, as reported by Guy Virtue – 1910-1917 – was having to run the gauntlet of other school children (presumably those heading to Bickley Hall) on their way to and from Chislehurst station. According to documents I found while scanning drainage plans in the Bromley Historic Collections – just one of the joys of local history! – Rev. Johnson, the headmaster, was planning a new temporary structure for a schoolroom in February 1910. It was interesting to see his address at Hillside, next door. In 1913, two new classrooms, a music room, three new playgrounds and a gymnasium were added. The playing field was levelled. The boys were known to play (and lose) against girls' teams – maybe the girls at Coed-bel down the road?

When Abbey Lodge opened as a Red Cross hospital caring for the wounded from the Western Front in October 1914, Mr Alfred Spenser Johnson worked as an interpreter for the Belgian soldiers. The boys were also allowed to visit and practice their French on the patients. How painful might that have been?

Pupil numbers increased to 48 by September 1915, when the school left Lubbock Road and moved to some larger premises on Chislehurst Road; hence the name of the Bickley site today – St Hugh's Playing Fields.

Alfred Johnson died on Christmas Eve 1954, and I found his obituary in the Kentish Times. He had been joint headmaster of St Hugh's, with his brother the Rev, Johnson, for nearly 40 years. The Lubbock Road premises were described as 'modest' and he as 'requiring great self-confidence to make the move. The school honours board was studded with scholarships to the famous schools in the land. However, Alfred could also transmit his enthusiasm with equal skill to more backward children so that they too passed their examinations with surprising ease. Alfred's personal love of music more than anything else gave a stamp to students, how lively is every remembrance of him, vital, forthright, eccentric, enthusiastic, unforgettable and unforgotten.' The funeral service took place at St Nicholas Church, followed by interment at Chislehurst Cemetery.

I am rather horrified, as I write the chapter on St Hugh's, to see that it has been six years since I first contacted the owners of the four houses that now sit on the Lamas site! There seemed little harm in putting a note through these neighbours' doors, and I'm so glad I did. The response from one resident, Seren, turned into a great gossip over a glass of wine, and a new friendship. She had been meaning to do more research, but had found 'life' getting in the way. That seems to be true of my last six years, too.

Seren had books and documents relating to the Mount Zion era of her home. She told me that the Mount Zion name was in the documents relating to the newly-built houses in 1962. When it was Mount Zion, it was a children's home run by the Barbican Mission to the Jews, a society dedicated to saving Jews from being Jewish. The same group of carers who had begun their work at Seven Trees down the road. Several of the children were refugees from war-torn Europe; others were abandoned children, whose mothers had given birth to them in prison or other desperate circumstances. Parents had to sign an agreement committing their children to the home until they were 16, and permitting the children to be brought up in the Christian faith.

The carers' 'aunties' were all committed Christians, dedicated to saving souls. They came from all over the country, having been recruited through the Mission's work in other cities. They attended Christ Church on Sunday evenings. At Mount Zion, wide, white steps led up to the glass doors and into the hall, the very same steps on which Ellen Lubbock had entertained the X Club. On the right was the girls' sitting room, half the size of the boys' common room, which was next door. The house apparently felt like a stately home, with brass door knobs and finger panels. In each room was a bell that in years past had summoned servants to Ellen Lubbock or Caroline Johnston. There was a basement with many rooms, including a boot hole where all the shoes were kept. The pantry had one whole wall lined with a huge dresser. The kitchen was enormous, with a low ceiling and small windows. The dining room was also in the basement, a long room that ran the length of one side of the house.

Upstairs was the prayer room. An enclosed bridge ran from the first floor of the main house to the staff annexe, behind which was a small chapel; on the other side of the house was a large wooden building used as a gym.

One story drew my particular attention. Andrew, Teddy Albert and Thelma Perkins were placed as small children in Mount Zion. They knew little of their mother, the daughter of a Jewish refugee from Russia, and of their father they only knew he came from the Caribbean. The story of the quest of the Perkins family *In search of Mr McKenzie* was published in 1991 by the Women's Press, and gives wonderful insight into life in the children's home. Thelma's strongest memories are of being saved on a Sunday in order to go to heaven. The children sat quietly colouring Christian texts – 'Though your sins be scarlet, they shall be white as snow' – and she sang, 'O wash me in the blood of the lamb, and I shall be whiter than snow.' This little black girl with short curly hair wondered if she really would turn white!

The late Isobel Hider was matron in 1951, working for Rev. Stephen Leveson, who had originally been a boy in the home. She recalled the library for the children containing the Just William stories of local author Richmal Crompton. Mr R. Dungate recalls having Teddy McKenzie in his Boys' Brigade class, possibly the first child of colour encountered in Chislehurst. In 1953, the Brigade attended the Royal Albert Hall, and Andrew featured prominently on the TV broadcast.

Mount Zion flourished until 1960, becoming a general children's home. It eventually closed and Lamas finally fell to the demolition bulldozer. The history of the Lubbocks, Johnstons, St Hugh's boys and several orphaned children had come to an end, but the stories live on.

St Hugh's school photo 1913

William Willett's Coach House and stables

19. The Flood

1968
Chalk quarry, William Willett and the Rising Kyd

My stories of the road cannot be finished without including the unfortunate flooding of 1968.

In the spring of 2015, I was delighted to receive e-mail correspondence from Jillian Turner and her sister Susan, one-time residents of Lubbock Road. They wanted to purchase a copy of the Heritage Lottery funded Camden Place map, and fortuitously for me, come and visit, to tell me their childhood recollections of the road. Better get the kettle on!

They had grown up at number 11, Cotleigh, which was next to the Coach House, the original stables of William Willett. They were also the children who escaped the 1968 floods by boat from their top floor window! Sadly, their father, Tony Turner – Chislehurst Society Road Steward during the 1980s and 90s and Chairman of the Kyd Brook Flood Liaison Committee – died at the end of March that year, aged 92. Lubbock Road residents today are most fortunate that Tony worked so hard on this project and managed to get proper flood defences in place at the lower part of the road.

It was Tony who told the girls that chalk from Chislehurst had been used by Sir Christopher Wren in the building of St Paul's Cathedral – not something I can authenticate, but a lovely legend. Jillian and Susan also told me of a Danish writer, Mr Dahn – pseudonym John Holgate – who lived at 109, and wrote a book called *How to make a Cow Laugh* – now, there's an idea!

Cotleigh was built by Mr Carter, a ship's carpenter from Bude, for himself to live in. Cotleigh is a small village in Devon, hence the rationale for the name of his house. The house is deeper on the plot, since the site included the entrance to the builder's yard at the back. It took ten years to build, starting in 1928; and Carter also built numbers 1, 3, 5, 7 and 9. The houses were renumbered in 1956, and number 7 became number 11 – not sure I can get my head around that! The craftsmanship of the building was highly regarded, particularly the use of seasoned pine for the loft and, most importantly, for the floor. Despite being submerged for at least 24 hours in the flood, the floorboards did not buckle or twist. Perhaps Mr Carter was the modern-day equivalent of Noah!

Mr Carter worked for William Willett. Mr Carter stayed with this firm for 23 years, later taking over what became the local branch in Lubbock Road. At one time, he was involved in renovating the stables at Buckingham Palace.

One further pleasurable diversion in this correspondence was that a follower of my Friel on Friday YouTube channel, Janice, turned out to be the grand-daughter of Mr Carter. She now lives in Holland, but I was able to put her in touch with the Turners. They exchanged e-mails about white gates and Albertine roses – the heady atmosphere of childhood days.

Janice's family moved to the end house in the road, Finchdale, and one of her earliest vivid memories is of looking out of the bedroom window at the front of the house towards the railway, and seeing an army tank on the top of a low freight carrier, being pulled by a steam engine, c. 1951.

On 15 September 1968, excessive rainfall created the unusual event of the Thames swelling and flowing backwards. The nearby tributaries could not cope and overflowed. The Kyd Brook started rising across Lubbock Road during the morning. The Turners and several other residents started taking their possessions upstairs. They even saw a squirrel on the railway bank opposite, carrying its young, one at a time, from the bottom of the bank to near the top.

Water came under the front door from about lunchtime, and the Turner girls counted gradually as it crept up each stair, to reach a depth of six feet inside the house. The electricity substation opposite blew up. Rescue boats had been organised, and the four Turners, plus their Alsatian, were rescued out of the landing window. They were taken up the road as far as number 23, where the water had stopped. Christ Church parishioners were asked to help out with accommodation.

The man living in The White House, the last bungalow in Lubbock Road before entering Lower Camden, was in his living room, when the floodwater entered so fast that he was unable to open his door to escape – and he was briefly pinned to his ceiling!

The water stayed for five days and then suddenly receded, flowing down the driveway between Cotleigh and the Coach House. It was widely believed that water must have gone through the chalk in the old quarry at the back of the house; after the flood, the land above it did slip. The landslip took away the footpath inexplicably known as the Kangaroo Walk, which originally stretched all the way from Old Hill to Finchdale at number 1 Lubbock Road.

Another resident tells the story from the perspective of being absent at

The Turner children in the quarry garden

Winter at Cotleigh

Lower Camden chalk quarry

Lower Camden chalk quarry

the time of the event, and arriving back to the devastation. Mr McKenzie, a high-ranking civil servant, who worked on the Beveridge Report in the 1940s and later wrote his memoirs about his government work during the Second World War, recalls, 'Our next-door neighbours met us at the station lest we receive too big a shock. The house was indescribably filthy and chaotic but humidifiers had been installed by Borough Engineers. The London Electricity Board said the power system could not be used and would need a complete rewire, the work was reminiscent of the blitz! Contrast that with the local gas fitter who arrived on his bicycle and reconnected the gas within an hour! The telephone was out of action leading to a curious irrational feeling of isolation and loneliness, soon dispelled by a conversation with a party of telephone engineers, working in a manhole opposite, who rang with the welcome news that the line was reinstalled. They had worked every day, including Sunday. We spent the afternoons and meal times with neighbours. The local Red Cross and Bromley Social Services made an impression, the lady officer of the Red Cross was indefatigable in scrubbing floors and discarding contaminated foodstuffs into a horrid heap on the front lawn.

'The abiding memory of living in a flood damaged house for 8 months was the difficulty of finding things, it was as if one were always engaged in moving house while yet ending up still in the same one'.

There was another flood in 1977, and number 11 was flooded to the front doorstep. The event had a noticeable effect in welding a number of individual householders into a community of good neighbours.

Tony Turner helped to create the Kyd Brook Flood Liaison Committee, which established a phone-linked warning system. The Department for Environment Food & Rural Affairs still contacts low-lying houses in the road to raise the alarm of potential floods. The waterway in Lower Camden was widened and deepened near the Lubbock Road junction. Grilles and sumps have been put in upstream, to catch debris, and regular inspections take place. Tony's contribution to the safety and ambience of the road cannot be underestimated.

Jillian and Susan also remembered that there used to be a phone box at the lowest end of Lubbock Road, opposite Camden Park Road, until 1961. In the back garden of Cotleigh, when gardening in the 1960s, they found several old clay pipes, which may have been smoked by the men who built the railway opposite, or by chalk miners in the quarry.

I have been pleased to receive information from recent graffiti surveys undertaken in the old chalk pit but sad not to see the name of Nathaniel Strode on the list of scrawled names. You'd think he'd have made an inspection of his property, underground or otherwise!

Chalk Mine at Lower Camden, Chislehurst

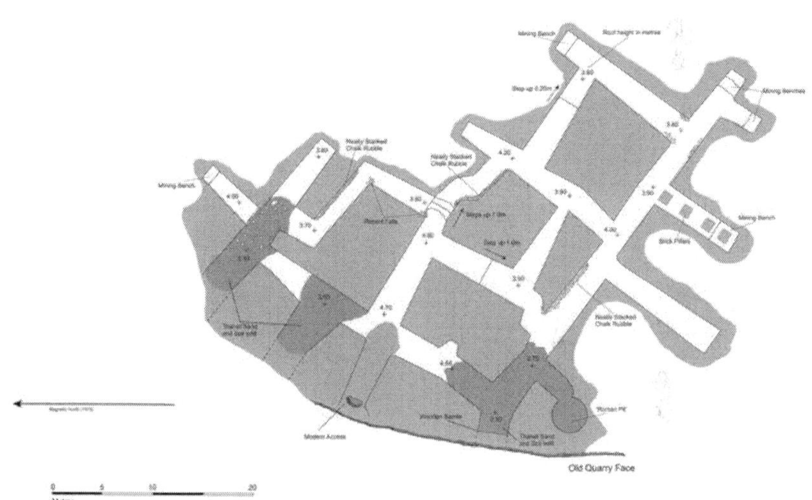

Hatton Cottage 1906

Conclusions

At the End of the Road

There have been as many frustrations in my research as there have been exciting finds, particularly the day I accidentally deleted some precious writing, never to recover it! But as I approached the thinner end of my research, I realised it coincided with the northern end of the road, where several of the houses had failed to throw up distinctive stories.

23 and 27 Lubbock Road are captured in an old photograph. This terraced group of three houses were designed by Ernest Newton around 1908, cleverly they look like one house with two gabled end wings. The photo sums up the calm, almost rural nature of the road in the era before the First World War. How atmospheres change; although the road is part of the wider Chislehurst Conservation Area, it isn't exactly calm today. Cars speed through aiming to avoid the A222 en route to Bromley or Sidcup and parked cars don't seem to slow them down that much!

Then there is Hatton Cottage, probably the most picturesque house in the road. Described as a fantasy house in *Discover Chislehurst*, but incorrectly written as dating back to 1857 – in documents about listing in the Conservation Area, which I have seen. (The 1857 date actually refers to the find of Roman pottery in the chalk below the 'cottage'). I had seen images of the house from 1906 in *The Builder* magazine, showing the architect to be Arthur Heron Ryan-Tenison (also the designer of the Submariners' Monument on the Thames Embankment), but he wasn't born until 1880, so he could hardly have designed this house before he was born! At least I can set the record straight to that extent. Other than Percy Straus who lived there during the First World War, I have not been able to learn more about the house's heritage. Yvonne Auld tells of Percy resigning from the Chislehurst Urban District Council in 1916 on account of his German name. Percy was in fact British by birth (his father was naturalised about 1847) and had a son fighting for his country but he felt it was 'impossible for anyone with any connection with Germany to take a leading part in public affairs'. Such a shame, as a capable accountant his skills were much missed, but at least Abbey Lodge hospital was the beneficiary of his newly available time.

Hatton House, nearby, is now the site of Hatton Court, a double block of flats. Hatton House was quite a size. I did find outline plans of the property when going through the drainage plans in the Bromley Historic Collections but, sadly, no actual picture. Some names did emerge: in 1887, the family of William Mawe, a draper from the North of England and related by marriage to the Woods at Camden Lodge. When his widow, Hannah, died in 1914, she was worth £44,000, some of which was left to her sculptress daughter, Annie.

As of the 1901 census, Edward Fooks, a solicitor, lived there. Naturally, I contacted the law firm bearing the name Fooks, but their archives have long been lost in various mergers, so no photograph of the founding lawyer came to light. I was sent photographs of the lodge or gardener's house, which are charming, but revealed more of the size of Coed-bel than anything else.

Finally, the Fehr family, about which there is mention in *Edwardian Chislehurst*. Arthur Battle comments that: 'long after the car had become every man's method of transport Mr and Mrs Fehr still went abroad in a "victoria", a light four wheeled horse-drawn carriage with an elevated driver's seat up front'. And indeed, during the bombing raids of the Second World War, Mr Fehr's victoria could be seen with old Egglesfield, the coachman, his top hat on the seat beside him, a tin hat on his head with a flying bomb roaring across the sky. There's loyalty for you. A corner of the original Hatton House came to light in a photograph of Mrs Fehr going in her carriage to the election of Pat Hornsby-Smith in 1970!

Talking of drainage brings me to the tale of the Coach House at the junction with Lower Camden. These were originally the stables of William Willett, the time lord who introduced the concept of Daylight Saving Time to the UK. This is an attractive building, with its round window and the central gable, which was most likely for a hoist. The clock on the roof does not work: how ironic, for the man who set about changing the clocks! The building was designed for Willett by his consulting architect, Ernest Newton in 1909, and is today split into four separate dwellings.

Following a fascinating climb – or should I say pull, as I was helped right up to the top of the landscape, with no little effort – to see the old tennis court layout at Hatton Court, my accomplice that day – Alison, from Willow Lodge – remembered that she knew one of the owners of the stable block forming numbers 13 – 19 Lubbock Road today. Obviously, we immediately went to knock at his door. I'm pleased to say we were warmly greeted and, indeed, invited to take a closer look. 'Would you like to see my drain cover?' said Jeremy, the owner. Not one to turn down such an invitation, I'm delighted to report a great find. There, on the drain

23-27 Lubbock Road, designed by Ernest Newton

Mrs Fehr of Hatton House, boarding her carriage in 1970

Gardeners' Lodge at Hatton House

Willett draincover behind the Coach House

Kincraig pillar beside Christ Church

Two views of Kincraig

Lubbock Road today...

...has it changed that much?

cover, indelibly marked in the metal, were the letters Wm. Willett – real provenance, because, of course, Willett had his own building firm, and here was the evidence of his endeavours. That story has been told with some alacrity at various talks locally.

There are houses whose past still elude me. Thorndale is one. In 2013, I was contacted by David Hurst, searching for the home of his great-grandfather (c.1896), William Rees Powell. His enquiry came via the Chislehurst Library, and I was pleased to be able to show David where the house had once been. He had records of his ancestor travelling back to the UK from South Africa, where he had been a consulting engineer with the Natal Steam Coal Company and had, according to his obituary in the Johannesburg Star, bought an 'estate' in Chislehurst. I'm not sure Thorndale equates to an 'estate' – certainly not by the standards of Nathaniel Strode – but it does now house several flats, so it cannot have been small. I still haven't found a picture of the house, but I did spend a pleasant afternoon with David and his mother.

Kincraig holds a fascination for me, mostly due to the very ancient stone gatepost immediately next to that of Christ Church. The first occupant, James Cruickshank, named the house Kincraig, after a place just south of Aviemore in the Highlands of Scotland. Cruickshank lived in Lubbock Road in 1887; he was a hay factor agent from Edinburgh. I have been given a picture of the house by a wonderful postcard researcher, Ken Speers, but no more has come to light.

The houses merely named Miss Munro on the 1890 map turned out to be 'Selwyns', now long gone. Miss Munro was the daughter of a King's Bench barrister, who had in turn died in Madeira. Isabel Munro died in 1913, and, soon after her, so did an era.

But it's never the end, is it? When I'm not actually looking – and more than likely it will happen that, just as I go to press, a never-before-seen picture will come to light, or someone will send an e-mail from across the globe – and I will see the research trail stretching out further. I'm very glad to say that history keeps on giving, and this Lubbock Road journey might just be volume one!